Florida

Hometown Cookbook

Pensacola Beach

Florida

Hometown Cookbook

by Sheila Simmons & Kent Whitaker

GreatAmericanPublishers.com · 888·854·5954

978-1-934817-46-9

First Edition

10 9 8 7 6 5 4 3 2 1

Great American
COOKBOOKS

a subsidiary of:

Great American Publishers
171 Lone Pine Church Road • Lena, MS 39094
TOLL-FREE 1.888.854.5954 • www.GreatAmericanPublishers.com

by Sheila Simmons & Kent Whitaker

Contents

Tampa Skyline

Introduction

Welcome to The Sunshine State and the eighth addition to the STATE HOMETOWN COOKBOOK SERIES—*Florida Hometown Cookbook*! From beautiful white sand beaches to theme parks and race tracks to the Everglades, Florida is teeming with fun. In addition to its range of varied vacation destinations, Florida is home to a diverse mix of people from many places, which is reflected in her food.

A wide range of cultures has influenced the basic Spanish and Southern cuisine of the state. From *Chipotle Shrimp Fillo Cups* to *Florida Wildflower Honey-Glazed Carrots* to *Key Lime Fudge*, you'll enjoy a delicious taste of Florida in every chapter.

From *Triple Citrus Salmon*, *Ham & Chicken Wraps*, and *Crabby Potato Soup* to *Pull-Apart Cheddar-Bacon Ranch Bread*, *Easy Homestead-Miami Spanish-Style Rice*, and *Orange Pecan Pie*, easy-to-follow recipes make it simple to cook delicious dishes your family will love.

As a prime vacation spot, Florida has a lot to offer families. Everyone from lifelong Floridians to new residents and even occasional visitors will enjoy the many fun festivals held across the state. From the **Barberville Strawberry Fest** to Key West's **Key Lime Festival** and the **South Florida Garlic Fest** in Lake Worth to the **Apalachicola Oyster Cook-Off**, there's a celebration for everyone to enjoy when traveling The Sunshine State.

Kent and I both dedicate this book to our spouses. Kent says, "I want to dedicate this book to my wife, Allyson Whitaker. She loves Florida as much as I do. I could not imagine doing the roadwork, research, and recipe testing in The Sunshine State with a better companion. When not working on the book, we took in the state with our loving pups. We had a blast!"

My husband, Roger, and I love to travel, and when he has the pick, we're Florida beach bound every time. His love of Florida is contagious. Researching this book got us off the beach and into the heart of Florida to learn more about the people and the food. The more we learned, the greater our appreciation grew for the beautiful Sunshine State. Thank you, Roger, for the fun we have in our travels and in the day-to-day running of our businesses and our families. You are the best.

As with every book in the series, the Florida edition wouldn't be possible without the help of a whole bunch of people, including family, friends, and people we've met along the way. Kent says, "Allyson and I wish to send special thanks and prayers to all of the wonderful friends and neighbors who we've come to know and cherish in our adopted Florida towns of Mexico Beach, Port St. Joe, Cape San Blas, St. Teresa, and Alligator Point. Many locals and family members from the area have helped us with several book projects over the years. Our hearts go out following the devastation from Hurricane Michael. I hope this collection of recipes and stories helps preserve some local culinary history. We can't wait to visit with you again."

We also want to thank the wonderful people associated with the festivals featured in this book. You were all so helpful and generous with your time. Our sincerest appreciation also goes to Nichole Stewart, Zak Simmons, and Anita Musgrove. You are the best production team around. Thank you, Brooke and Diane, for keeping things running while we research, and Christy Campbell, Amber Feiock, Tiffany Gant, Tasha Monk, and Kristen Parker for ensuring our books make it out into the world.

We sincerely hope you enjoy this delightful taste of Florida as much as we enjoyed researching and writing it. Now, if you'll excuse us, we are headed to the beach.

Wishing you many happy kitchen memories,

Sheila Simmons & Kent Whitaker

Even youths grow tired and weary, and young men stumble and fall; but those who hope in the LORD will renew their strength. They will soar on wings like eagles; they will run and not grow weary, they will walk and not be faint.

—Isaiah 40:30-31

Beverages & Appetizers

Fort Myers

Apple-Peanut Butter Smoothie

Everyone loves apple slices smeared with peanut butter, so we used the same delicious flavors to create this smoothie. And it's quick…only about five minutes from beginning to end. Makes one serving so double as needed.

1 cup milk
½ cup peeled, shredded apple
3 tablespoons creamy peanut butter
1 tablespoon ground flaxseeds
1 tablespoon maple syrup or honey

Using a blender, combine milk, apple, peanut butter, flaxseeds and syrup. Cover and blend until combined. Pour into a 14- to 18-ounce glass. Serve immediately.

Florida Dairy Farmers, Altamonte Springs

Citrus Dream Milkshake

Delicious and easy. Add your favorite spirit to make this an adult summertime treat.

> ½ ounce (about 4½ tablespoons) natural sugar
> 4 ounces Florida grapefruit juice
> 4 ounces Florida orange juice
> 2 drops natural vanilla extract
> 4 ounces low-fat milk

Combine all ingredients in a blender with 2 ounces (approximately 4 cups) ice. Blend until smooth. Pour into a glass, add a straw and serve. Garnish with sliced fruit, if desired.

www.freshfromflorida.com

Alicia's Sausage Dip

I use a local brand of ground sausage with a spicy kick. I suggest you do the same for extra taste. Don't drain the Rotel as the dip needs that extra moisture.

> 1 pound ground pork sausage
> 1 (8-ounce) package cream cheese, softened
> 1 (10-ounce) can Rotel tomatoes with juice
> ½ cup diced green onion
> ½ cup diced cilantro

In a deep skillet over medium heat, brown and crumble sausage; drain. Stir in cream cheese, Rotel, onion and cilantro; stir over low heat until mixed well. Serve warm, or even chilled, with tortilla chips.

Alicia Imperial Lankford, Jacksonville

Cheese & Chili Dip

This very simple recipe can be made in the oven or on the grill in a foil pan as well as in the microwave.

> 1 (8-ounce) package cream cheese, softened
> 1 (15-ounce) can chili without beans
> 1 cup finely shredded Cheddar cheese
> 1 green onion, chopped

Spread cream cheese onto bottom of a microwave-safe pie pan. Top with chili then cheese. Microwave on high 1 to 2 minutes or until dip is hot and cheese is melted. Sprinkle with onion. Serve hot with chips for dipping.

Damon Barfield, Green Cove Springs

Diggy's Over-the-Top Cheese Dip

> 1 pound ground Italian sausage
> 1 (15-ounce) can whole-kernel corn
> 2 (15-ounce) cans Rotel tomatoes
> 1 (16-ounce) package Velveeta, cubed
> 1 (8-ounce) package cream cheese
> Additional spices as desired

Brown sausage in a large nonstick saucepan; drain. Return to saucepan and add remaining ingredients. Cook over low heat, stirring frequently, until cheeses are melted. This is also perfect for slow cookers.

Diggy Moore, Coco Beach

Christine's Pepper Jelly Dipping Sauce

1 (8-ounce) package cream cheese, softened
1 cup pepper jelly
¼ cup water or milk

Combine cream cheese and pepper jelly in a nonstick saucepan over low heat until soft. Stir in water or milk and mix well before removing from heat. Serve warm.

Christine Morgan, Pensacola and Panama City

Dunedin Orange Festival

Dunedin • July

Dunedin Orange Festival celebrates the history of the citrus industry in Dunedin. From the early 1880s to the 1950s, Dunedin enjoyed a bustling orange business. In 2009, local artist and resident Steven Spathelf and Marsha Goins secretly painted loose oranges around downtown and waited for the public response. Locals, visitors, and media alike came to see the oranges. Shortly after, the first annual Dunedin Orange Festival was organized by local businesses, the historical museum, and the Dunedin Chamber of Commerce to boost summer business and revisit the town's history with the orange industry.

51 Main Street • Dunedin, FL 34698
727.736.1176 • www.dunedinorangefestival.com
Facebook: Dunedin Orange Festival

Classic Crab Dip

2 cups cooked and flaked crab
¼ cup mayonnaise
2 tablespoons sour cream
2 teaspoons seafood seasoning
2 teaspoons hot sauce
2 teaspoons Worcestershire sauce or to taste

Combine all ingredients in a bowl and mix until crabmeat is broken up. Use a fork (or even a food processor) if you want a creamier dip. Cover and allow it to rest in your refrigerator an hour or more before serving. Taste and add additional seasonings and Worcestershire, if desired.

Michael Whitfield, Jacksonville

Wellington Bacon & Bourbon Fest

Wellington • 3rd Weekend in March

The Wellington Bacon & Bourbon Fest celebrates the most loved food in the universe, bacon, and the quintessential American liquor, bourbon. The two-day event features live music, artists and crafters, an eclectic menu of bacon-infused culinary delights, and a collection of over forty bourbons and whiskeys for your tasting pleasure. The Fest also offers participants extensive bacon and bourbon pairing seminars, including an exclusive Pappy Van Winkle tasting. Our menu of bacon and pork related dishes includes everything from the sublime Forever Roasted Bourbon BBQ Pork & Bacon Sandwich to the insane Bacon Bar, featuring chocolate-covered and caramel nut–dipped bacon and bacon desserts. We'll have plenty of backyard games, cornhole, Jenga, checkers, and the infamous pig races! We've cleared it with your doctor, your cardiologist, and your mother; enjoy life at the Wellington Beach Bacon & Bourbon Fest.

12100 Forest Hill Boulevard • Wellington, FL 33414
561.279.0907 • www.baconbourbonfest.com
Facebook: BaconBourbonFest

Uncle Charles' Dilled Shrimp Dip

"My wife, Ally, likes to say she married me because my cooking reminds her of her Uncle Charles. Here is his original recipe for Dilled Shrimp Dip. Enjoy."

—Kent Whitaker, Author

½ pound fresh shrimp
1 (8-ounce) package cream cheese, softened
1 tablespoon mayonnaise
½ teaspoon garlic powder
1 tablespoon ketchup
1½ teaspoons Worcestershire sauce
1 tablespoon grated onion
2 teaspoons dill weed

Cook shrimp in boiling water until pink, 2 to 3 minutes. Drain and cool under cold running water. Reserve 2 to 3 whole peeled shrimp for garnish. Peel and finely chop remaining shrimp. Combine with remaining ingredients. Place in a serving bowl, cover tightly and chill several hours or overnight. Garnish with reserved whole shrimp and serve.

Uncle Charles and Aunt Wynona Johnson, Tallahassee

Ranch Jalapeño Dip

Once you start eating this, it's hard to stop.

1 (16-ounce) container sour cream
1 (1-ounce) envelope ranch dip mix
2 large jalapeño or serrano peppers, deseeded and finely diced (leave seeds in if you want a real kick)
⅓ cup chopped fresh cilantro
1 to 2 green onions, finely chopped
1 lime, juiced
Milk, optional

Mix all ingredients (except milk) together. Use milk to thin dip if needed. Serve with Fritos, tortilla chips and/or veggies.

Laurie Paddack Wilkes, Fort Myers

Grilled Baby Corn Salsa

What I love most about this salsa is its mixture of textures and flavors. It is simple to throw together and great as a topping for tofu or any other protein you like.

- 1 (15-ounce) can baby corn, drained
- ½ sweet onion, quartered
- 2 tomatoes, halved
- 1 whole jalapeño, optional
- Olive oil mister
- ⅛ teaspoon sea salt
- 2 tablespoons freshly chopped cilantro
- 1 lime

Preheat grill to medium high; place a grate cover on grill grates so corn will not fall through. Spray veggies with olive oil. Place all veggies on heated grill and cook until char marks appear. Flip once and grill until char marks appear on second side. Remove from heat; cool 5 minutes. Chop veggies into bite-size pieces. For no heat, don't use the jalapeño; to add heat, add a small amount of jalapeño at a time until desired level of heat is reached. Mix or combine in a bowl and sprinkle with salt and cilantro; finish with a squeeze of fresh lime.

Dawn Hutchins, St. Johns
Florida Coastal Cooking & Wellness

Cantaloupe Salsa

1 cup diced cantaloupe
3 tablespoons chopped green onion
1 red bell pepper, chopped
3 sprigs cilantro, chopped
1 tablespoon lime juice
Pinch salt
Pinch hot pepper flakes

In large bowl, mix ingredients together and chill. Serves 4.

Avocado-Tomato Salsa

½ cup cubed avocado, ½-inch cubes
¼ cup cubed tomato, ½-inch cubes
⅛ cup sliced green bell pepper, ¼-inch slices
¼ teaspoon kosher salt
1 teaspoon black pepper
1 tablespoon fresh lime juice
½ teaspoon chopped fresh cilantro
½ teaspoon hot sauce

Combine all ingredients in a bowl, cover and refrigerate 15 minutes before serving.

Chef Eileen Morris, Crystal Beach
www.personalcheftampabay.com

Mango Cheese Fondue

1 (8-ounce) package French Brie cheese, top crust removed
4 to 6 ounces Jacquie's Jamming Fabulous Mango Jam
⅓ cup crushed nuts

Preheat oven to 375°. Place Brie in a baking dish; bake 10 minutes to soften. Remove from oven and spread Jacquie's Mango Jam over the whole top. Sprinkle with nuts. Return to oven for 10 to 15 minutes, until cheese melts. Serve hot with crackers or crispy French bread.

Jacquie Hoare-Ward, Naples
Jacquie's Jamming Jams

Tampa Bay's Tailgate Taste Fest

Tampa • 1st Saturday in October

Tampa Bay's Tailgate Taste Fest is the ultimate place to be in October. A free family-friendly event, Tailgate Taste Fest's robust schedule includes entertainment for the casual event-goer and the ultimate football fan alike. Entertainment consists of a food competition with local restaurants serving up the most delicious tailgate foods Tampa has to offer. You'll also enjoy live music from the best local bands, a competitive cornhole tournament, and of course, live action from the day's most exciting college football games on large LED video screens.

Curtis Hixon Waterfront Park
600 North Ashley Drive • Tampa, FL 33602
813.342.4065 • www.tailgatetastefest.com
Facebook: TailgateTasteFest

Stone Church Pâté

This is the best ever pâté.

1 pound chicken livers
⅔ cup milk
⅓ cup port wine
2 tablespoons olive oil
1 medium onion, finely chopped
½ carrot, skinned and diced
1 stalk celery, diced
1 apple, cored and chopped (skin on)
1 pear, cored and chopped (skin on)
¼ cup brandy
2 tablespoons white wine
1 cup apple juice
Vegetable oil for frying
Salt and pepper to taste
1 teaspoon thyme
½ pound butter, softened

Rinse chicken livers in colander; drain as thoroughly as possible. Place in a bowl and cover with milk and port wine; soak in refrigerator at least 4 hours (preferably overnight). Heat olive oil in a skillet over medium-high heat. Add onion and cook until golden brown. Add carrot, celery, apple and pear; cook until tender. Add brandy, white wine and apple juice; place in blender. In a skillet, add livers to very hot vegetable oil (not olive oil). Do not stir at first, allowing livers to caramelize from the heat; add salt and pepper to taste. Stir after caramelization starts; remove from heat when cooked. Add livers to vegetable mixture in blender. Add thyme and butter; process till smooth. Taste; if gritty, add more butter. Serve with toast points or crackers. Freezes well. Serves 10.

Sue Dannahower, Fort Pierce

Stuffed Mushrooms

These mushrooms are too good for words and very easy to make! They are my favorite stuffed mushroom.

48 medium-size mushroom caps
4 tablespoons olive oil
4 tablespoons butter
2 cups finely chopped onions
8 tablespoons chopped pecans
4 cloves garlic, chopped
10 ounces spinach
8 ounces feta cheese, crumbled
8 ounces Gruyère cheese, grated
8 tablespoons chopped fresh dill
Salt and pepper to taste

Remove stems from mushrooms and save for another use. Wash mushrooms. Heat oil and butter in skillet. Add onion and cook until tender. Preheat oven 400°. Add pecans and garlic to onion and cook for one minute. Add spinach and cook 5 minutes. Add cheese, dill, salt and pepper. Arrange mushroom caps, cavity side up in a baking dish. Spoon the spinach-cheese mixture into each mushroom cap. Bake 8 to 10 minutes. Serve immediately.

Baked Artichoke "Crab" Cakes with Easy Vegan Tartar Sauce

My baked artichoke "crab" cakes are vegan and gluten free. They have less fat than the usual crab cake and are packed with flavor.

Tartar Sauce:
- ⅓ cup vegan mayonnaise
- 2 teaspoons lemon juice
- 2 teaspoons coarse-ground prepared mustard

Cakes:
- 2 (15-ounce) cans artichoke hearts, drained and rinsed
- 1 cup gluten-free breadcrumbs
- 2 green onions, chopped
- ¼ cup corn kernels, fresh or frozen
- ¼ cup chopped veggie mixture (I use red cabbage, red onion and bell pepper)
- Handful chopped parsley
- 2 teaspoons Old Bay seasoning
- ½ teaspoon garlic powder
- Salt and pepper to taste
- Coconut oil for greasing baking sheet

Preheat oven to 375°. Mix tartar sauce ingredients; refrigerate until ready to serve. In a food processor, pulse artichoke hearts a few times—just until crabmeat-like in texture, but not puréed. In a large bowl, stir together artichoke hearts, breadcrumbs, green onions, corn, veggies, parsley, Old Bay, garlic powder, salt and pepper. Stir until just combined; form into cakes. Place on a baking sheet greased with coconut oil. Bake 25 minutes flipping halfway through. Serve topped with Tartar Sauce.

Dawn Hutchins, St. Johns
Florida Coastal Cooking & Wellness

Bacon-Wrapped Tater Tot Bombs

You can never go wrong with bacon. These little bombs are a huge hit with my family and friends. When I make them, I usually double or triple the recipe and they are still gone within thirty minutes.

2 cups frozen tater tots, thawed
1 ounce sharp Cheddar cheese, cut into ¼-inch squares
4 slices bacon, quartered (depending on bacon, you may have to cut in thirds)
¼ cup packed brown sugar

Preheat oven to 400°. Line a baking sheet with parchment paper. Working 1 at a time, wrap each tater tot and cheese square in a piece of bacon. Dredge each in brown sugar, pressing to coat. Place tater tots, seam side down, onto baking sheet. Bake 20 to 25 minutes turning halfway through. Serve immediately.

Laurie Paddack Wilkes, Fort Myers

Fort Myers Beach Pier

Chicken Tortillas

Oil
1 (8-ounce) boneless, skinless chicken breast
1 teaspoon blackened seasoning
¾ cup plain yogurt
1½ teaspoons lime zest
2 tablespoons lime juice
¼ teaspoon salt
⅛ teaspoon pepper
1 cup peeled and finely chopped mango
⅓ cup finely chopped red onion
4 (8-inch) flour tortillas
½ cup crumbled blue cheese
2 tablespoons minced fresh cilantro

Lightly oil grill rack and set grill to medium heat. Sprinkle chicken with blackened seasoning. Grill chicken, covered, 6 to 8 minutes on each side or until a thermometer inserted into breast reads 165°; set aside to cool slightly. In a small bowl, mix yogurt, lime zest, lime juice, salt and pepper. Finely chop chicken and transfer to a small bowl; stir in mango and onion. Grill tortillas, uncovered, 2 to 3 minutes or until puffed. Flip tortillas, then top with chicken mixture and blue cheese. Grill, covered, 2 to 3 minutes longer or until bottoms of tortillas are lightly browned. Drizzle with yogurt mixture and sprinkle with cilantro. Cut each tortilla into four wedges.

Cheesy Chicken & Bacon Quesadilla with Yogurt Veggie Dip

The creamy Yogurt Veggie Dip is a perfect addition to this Cheesy Chicken and Bacon Quesadilla, and it makes a great dip for other dishes too.

Yogurt Veggie Dip:

2 cups plain Greek yogurt
1 (8-ounce) package frozen spinach, thawed, drained and chopped
½ cup grated Parmesan cheese
1 (1.8-ounce) envelope vegetable soup mix

In a medium bowl, combine dip ingredients, cover and refrigerate until ready to serve.

Quesadilla:

2 (9- to 10-inch) whole-wheat tortillas
1 chicken breast, cooked and chopped
2 tablespoons cooked and chopped bacon
½ cup Monterey Jack, colby or Mexican cheese
⅓ cup sliced bell pepper

Lightly coat a skillet with cooking spray. Place 1 tortilla in heated skillet. Top with chicken, bacon and cheese; place second tortilla on top. When cheese begins to melt and tortilla begins to crisp, flip to other side. Lightly brown second side; remove from skillet. Serve with Yogurt Veggie Dip and bell pepper.

Florida Dairy Farmers, Altamonte Springs

Cheesy Vegan Bean Quesadillas

This recipe is a family favorite. We make it at least once a week. If you have little ones around, like I do, this is one of the best ways to get them an amazing amount of protein. Hummus works beautifully in place of the cheese, especially if you have a fresh batch of hummus on hand.

4 gluten-free tortillas
High heat cooking spray or melted coconut oil
2 cups cooked black, red or white beans
4 tablespoons nutritional yeast
1 cup (or more) chopped kale
½ cup (or more) vegan shredded cheese
¼ to ½ teaspoon adobo seasoning

Preheat broiler. Treat tortillas with cooking spray or brush with coconut oil. Place 2 tortillas, oiled side down, on baking sheet; top each with half the remaining ingredients. Then top with remaining tortillas, oiled side up. Broil until top tortillas are crispy, about 3 minutes (watch carefully to prevent burning). Using a large spatula, flip each quesadilla to brown other side, about 3 minutes. Cool slightly, then slice and serve.

Dawn Hutchins, St. Johns
Florida Coastal Cooking & Wellness

Cuban Tostones

Tostones are actually fried green plantains, but you can use sweet plantains.

2 to 3 green plantains
Oil for frying
Salt

Peel and slice plantains into inch-long pieces (1½ inches at most). Heat oil in a frying pan; brown plantains on all sides. Remove from oil and allow to cool slightly so you can work with them. Mash each flat using a spatula or the bottom of a canned item. (Clean bottom of can first.) Gently refry flattened plantain pieces until they are even more golden. Remove from heat and sprinkle with salt. Serve immediately.

Heather Kirby, Fort Lauderdale

Chipotle Shrimp Fillo Cups

½ pound shrimp, cooked, peeled and coarsely chopped
1 yellow bell pepper, roasted, peeled and chopped
1 red bell pepper, roasted, peeled and chopped
½ cup chopped fresh cilantro
1 chipotle pepper in adobo sauce, deseeded and chopped
8 ounces grated Fontina cheese
2 (30-count) packages Athens Fillo Shells, defrosted

Preheat oven to 350°. In a large bowl, combine shrimp, peppers, cilantro, chipotle pepper and cheese. Place fillo shells on a baking sheet. Fill each cup with shrimp mixture; bake 7 to 10 minutes or until cheese is melted.

Sue Dannahower, Fort Pierce

Hushpuppy Grouper Poppers with Hot Tartar Sauce

Hot Tartar Sauce:
1½ cups mayonnaise
2 tablespoons finely chopped green onions
1½ tablespoons finely chopped jalapeño pepper
2 teaspoons hot sauce
2 teaspoons lemon juice
Salt and pepper to taste
Dash seafood seasoning

Combine all ingredients in a bowl. Cover and chill at least 1 hour before serving.

Hushpuppy Grouper Poppers:
1½ pounds grouper fillets
2 cups vegetable oil for frying
1 (8-ounce) package hushpuppy mix, plus ingredients to prepare per package directions
Flour for dredging

Cut grouper fillets in 1-inch-square pieces. Try to make them the same size and as evenly square as possible. (For hushpuppy fish sticks, cut the pieces longer.) Heat oil for frying. Prepare hushpuppy mix in a bowl per directions. Place a small amount of flour in a shallow dish or bowl. Dredge grouper pieces in flour and gently roll and dip in the hushpuppy mix coating evenly. Working in batches, fry in hot oil until golden brown. (It's best to cook a few at a time so that you can control the cooking times while being able to turn them. If you fry too many at once, you may end up with some burnt on one side or splash hot oil as you rush to try and turn them too quickly.) Dry on a rack over paper towels and serve hot with Hot Tartar Sauce for dipping.

Michael Whitfield, Jacksonville

Stuffed Jalapeños on the Grill

This recipe is a "must-try" if you like hot and spicy. It is a wonderful, fresh alternative to traditional jalapeño poppers that are breaded and deep-fried.

15 to 20 fresh jalapeño peppers
1 cup shredded Cheddar cheese
2 cups chopped fresh shrimp
½ cup fresh minced onion
1 pound sliced bacon

Cut off top of each pepper; remove core, seeds and veins. In a bowl, combine cheese, shrimp and onion; stuff each pepper with shrimp mixture. Cut each bacon slice in half; wrap each pepper. Skewer each pepper with a toothpick to hold bacon in place. Place peppers upright in grill-safe container (or use skewers and a metal rectangular cake pan); cook on outdoor grill 30 to 45 minutes or until peppers start to wrinkle and stuffing is bubbly.

Judie Mackie, Isle of Eight Flags Shrimp Festival

Speedy Chicken Nachos

This recipe is all about saving time and having a hot meal in a time pinch. You can use fresh chicken breasts, leftover chicken, or prepackaged and already cooked chicken. These are perfect for watching your favorite football team play or a quick main dish served up with Spanish rice and beans. It's versatile too as you can add as many different types of toppings as you wish.

2 (7-ounce) pouches Tyson chunk chicken breast
1 (1.25-ounce) envelope taco seasoning
1 (14-ounce) bag tortilla chips
1 (16-ounce) bag shredded Mexican-style cheese blend
1 (10-ounce) can Rotel tomatoes, drained
1 (2.25-ounce) can sliced black olives, drained

Preheat oven to broil. Place chicken in a bowl and top with half the taco seasoning. Using a fork, shred and mix chicken until well shredded and coated evenly with seasoning. (Use less taco seasoning for a mild flavor or more for a spicy flavor.) Arrange chips on a cookie sheet and cover with cheese. Top with Rotel tomatoes and seasoned chicken. Broil on top rack in oven about 3 minutes or until cheese starts to bubble. Remove from oven and top with black olives; broil 1 to 2 minutes longer until cheese if fully melted and chips and chicken are warmed through.

Lisa Barnes, Palm Beach

Palm Beach

Bread & Breakfast

Ocala National Forest

Sour Cream Banana Nut Loaf

I like to serve this bread warm, sliced, and with a scoop of ice cream. It's always popular and can be made with yogurt instead of sour cream.

½ cup butter, softened
1 cup sugar plus more for sprinkling
2 eggs
1½ cups flour
1 teaspoon baking soda
½ teaspoon salt
1 cup mashed bananas
½ cup sour cream
1 teaspoon vanilla extract
½ cup chopped nuts

Using an electric mixer, cream butter, sugar and eggs. In a separate bowl, combine flour, baking soda and salt. Add to creamed mixed and beat until well combined. Add mashed bananas, sour cream and vanilla and mix well. Stir in chopped nuts. Butter a medium-size loaf pan and sprinkle with sugar. Pour batter in pan and bake at 350° for 1 hour. Serve warm.

Karl Woda, Margate

Pull-Apart Cheddar-Bacon Ranch Bread

1 unsliced loaf sourdough bread (round is best)
8 to 12 ounces Cheddar cheese, thinly sliced
1 (3-ounce) package bacon bits
½ cup melted butter
1 tablespoon dry ranch dressing mix

Preheat oven to 350°. Using a sharp bread knife cut an X in the top of the bread, cutting deep but not through bottom crust. Place cheese slices inside cuts. Sprinkle bacon bits inside the cuts and over the bread. Combine butter and ranch dressing mix. Pour over bread. Wrap loaf in foil and place on baking sheet; bake 15 minutes. Unwrap and bake an additional 10 minutes or until cheese is melted.

Laurie Paddack Wilkes, Fort Myers

Fort Myers Beach Lions Club
Shrimp Festival

Lynn Hall Memorial Park • March

The Fort Myers Beach Lions Club Shrimp Festival is the major event of the year for Fort Myers Beach. The local Lions Club heads the events, including a parade, exhibition, queen's pageant, and the newly incorporated shrimp-eating contest! Drawing thousands of visitors from almost every state and many countries, the Lions Club Shrimp Festival is an event that locals count on year after year to put a smile on their faces and delicious "Pink Gold" shrimp dinners in their bellies, all while funding what serves to provide those less fortunate with opportunities they would otherwise not have.

950 Estero Boulevard • Fort Myers, FL 33931
239.454.0043 • www.fortmyersbeachshrimpfestival.com
Facebook: ShrimpFestFMB

Bacon Cornbread Stuffing

What's better than a hot pan of cornbread stuffing? Bacon, of course.
I suggest using thick-sliced bacon.

1 stick unsalted butter, divided (plus more to coat baking dish)
6 slices thick-cut bacon, chopped
4 onions, thinly sliced
4 celery stalks, chopped
1 tablespoon chopped fresh thyme
½ teaspoon kosher salt
½ teaspoon ground black pepper
3½ cups chicken stock, low sodium if you prefer
2 large eggs
¼ cup chopped parsley
4 scallions, thinly sliced
8 cups stale cornbread, ½-inch cubes
8 cups stale potato bread, ½-inch cubes
1 cup chopped pecans

Preheat oven to 375° and butter a 3-quart baking dish. Melt 6 tablespoons butter in a large pot over medium heat. Add bacon and onions; cook, stirring occasionally, until onions are soft and caramelized, about 5 minutes. Add celery, thyme, salt and pepper. Cook another 5 minutes or until celery is tender. Add chicken stock and bring to simmer. Whisk eggs, parsley and scallions in a large bowl. Stir in the cornbread and potato bread cubes; add pecans and vegetable mixture, stirring until combined. Transfer stuffing to prepared baking dish. Cut remaining 2 tablespoons butter into cubes and place over stuffing. Cover with foil and bake 30 minutes; uncover and bake until brown, about 20 minutes more.

Cindy Walker, Lakeland

Catur's Sweet Cornbread

I usually prefer plain cornbread but do like this sweet version which is exceptional served warm with butter melted on top. It's equally good cooked as muffins.

1 cup milk
¼ cup melted butter
1 large egg, beaten
1¼ cups yellow cornmeal
1 cup self-rising flour
½ cup sugar
½ teaspoon salt

Preheat oven to 400°. Treat a 9-inch-round pan with nonstick spray. In a bowl, beat milk, butter and egg; stir in remaining ingredients. The mixture should be a bit lumpy (you don't want pancake batter). Pour in pan and bake about 20 minutes or until golden brown on top. A toothpick inserted in the center should come out clean.

Catur Turnbull, Green Cove Springs

Bacon Jalapeño Hushpuppies

For this recipe, I like cooking real bacon and using a spoonful of the grease in the mix, but you can use store-bought bacon bits if you want. I've used store-bought jalapeño and freshly chopped; both are good, but don't use the store-bought jalapeño relish—it's too sweet.

4 to 6 slices bacon
2 large eggs, beaten
⅓ cup milk
¼ cup sugar
½ cup diced sweet onion

1½ tablespoons minced jalapeño pepper
1¼ cups self-rising flour
1¼ cups self-rising cornmeal
Pinch salt
Oil for frying

Cook bacon in a skillet over medium heat until crispy; drain, reserving 1 tablespoon drippings. Set aside to cool. In a large bowl, combine eggs, milk, sugar, onion and jalapeño; mix well. Crumble bacon and stir into batter along with reserved drippings. Blend in flour, cornmeal and salt. If the mixture is too dry, add just a few drops of milk. You want a thick, chunky mix. Drop by portions just a bit larger than a teaspoonful in preheated hot oil; fry until golden brown. Cook in small batches to keep oil hot. Drain on paper towels or a brown paper bag. Serve hot.

Jeff Collins, Hollywood

Self-Rising Hushpuppies

2 large eggs, beaten
⅓ cup milk
½ cup sugar
¼ cup diced sweet onion
1¼ cups self-rising flour
1¼ cups self-rising cornmeal
Pinch salt
Oil for frying

In a large bowl, combine eggs, milk, sugar and onion. Blend in flour, cornmeal and salt; mix well. Working in batches to keep the oil hot, drop by portions just a bit larger than a teaspoonful into hot oil; fry until golden brown. Drain on paper towels or a brown paper bag. Serve hot.

Jeff Collins, Hollywood

Cuban Flatbread Pork Pizza with Mojo Sauce

This Cuban-style pizza includes the same basic ingredients as a traditional Cuban sandwich—even dill pickles. Enjoy.

Mojo Pizza Sauce:

⅓ cup olive oil
⅓ cup orange juice
1½ tablespoons yellow mustard
1 tablespoon tomato paste or ketchup
½ tablespoon minced garlic
2 tablespoons lemon juice
1 teaspoon cumin powder
1 teaspoon salt
½ teaspoon cracked black pepper

Mix everything together in a bowl.

Flatbread Pizza:

2 deli flatbreads
Mojo Pizza Sauce
1 tablespoon tomato sauce or ketchup
1½ cups shredded mozzarella cheese
1½ cups shredded Swiss cheese
1 cup chopped cooked pork roast
½ cup dill pickle chips

Preheat oven to 450°. Place flatbreads on a cookie sheet. Cover with Mojo Pizza Sauce. Top with about half of each cheese plus pork and pickles. Top with remaining cheese. Bake about 10 minutes or until cheese is melted.

Heather Kirby, Fort Lauderdale

Dani's Mediterranean Artisan Pizza

Dani Hoy is a Trop-Rock musician and radio host in Key West. Her recipe for Mediterranean pizza features a yummy homemade crust.

Dough:

¾ cup warm water (105° to 115°)
1 (.75-ounce) envelope active dry yeast
3 tablespoons olive oil plus more for greasing bowl
2 cups all-purpose flour plus more for kneading dough
1 teaspoon sugar
¾ teaspoon salt

Pour warm water into a small bowl; stir in yeast. Let stand until yeast dissolves, about 5 minutes. Brush a large bowl lightly with olive oil. Mix 2 cups flour, sugar and salt in a food processor. Add yeast mixture and the 3 tablespoons olive oil; process until dough forms a sticky ball. Transfer to lightly floured surface. Knead dough about 1 minute or until smooth, adding more flour by tablespoonfuls if dough is very sticky. Transfer to prepared bowl; turn dough in bowl to coat with oil. Cover bowl with plastic wrap and let dough rise in warm, draft-free area until doubled in volume, about 1 hour. Punch down dough. (Dough may be used immediately. To work a day ahead, store in airtight container in refrigerator.) Roll out dough starting in center working outward toward edges until dough is your preferred size and thickness.

Pizza:

1½ tablespoon olive oil, divided
2 teaspoons fresh Italian herbs
2 teaspoons garlic powder or crushed red pepper
4 cups Italian six-cheese blend
2 teaspoons minced fresh basil
1 small tomato, thinly sliced
1 (2.25-ounce) can sliced black olives, drained
⅓ cup diced (or wedge sliced) onion, sautéed
2 to 3 small mushrooms, sliced and sautéed

Lightly coat top of shaped dough with ½ tablespoon olive oil. Sprinkle with Italian herbs and garlic powder. Top with cheese then layer with basil, tomato, black olives and sautéed onions and mushrooms. Bake on a pizza stone or cookie sheet at 400° for 15 to 20 minutes until cheese is melted and crust is browned. Remove from oven and cool slightly. Enjoy with a nice glass of red wine. Makes 1 large or 2 small pizzas depending on how you handle your dough.

Dani Hoy, Key West

Roasted Red Pepper Italian Sauce for Pizza

This recipe is simple and is great for pizza, spaghetti and so much more. Due to some medical issues my husband can't eat tomatoes for a while, but we love pizza. I decided to make a sauce like tomato sauce, minus the tomatoes.

5 red bell peppers
3 to 4 cloves garlic
1 teaspoon salt
1 teaspoon pepper or to taste
½ teaspoon Italian seasoning, optional

Slice peppers from top to bottom into about 6 wedge-shaped pieces. Lay on a nonstick cookie sheet and broil on middle rack until edges are browned. (Do not dry out as the moisture is needed.) While peppers are roasting, peel and mince garlic. Remove peppers from oven and place in food processor with remaining ingredients. Process until skin is completely broken up. Use a spoon to mix everything together and spread evenly over pizza crust.

Millie Johnson, Melbourne

Robert's Medianoche Sandwich

The Spanish word for midnight is *medianoche*. This Cuban sandwich became popular when it was served in Havana's legendary night clubs around midnight.

    4 sweet bread rolls (or egg bread or Challah)
    ¼ cup prepared mustard
    ¼ cup mayonnaise
    1 pound sliced Swiss cheese
    1 pound thinly sliced cooked ham
    1 pound thinly sliced fully cooked pork
    1 cup dill pickle slices
    ¼ cup melted butter

Split each roll in half horizontally. Spread mustard on the inside of the top and mayonnaise on the inside of the bottom of each roll. On bottom of each, layer cheese, ham and pork; top with pickles. Replace bread tops and brush outside of top and bottom with melted butter. Heat a sandwich press. (You can also use a George Forman Grill or heated skillet with a plate or burger press.) Press and cook 1 sandwich at a time 5 to 8 minutes or until outside is golden brown and cheese is melted. Slice and serve hot.

Robert Barrueco, Miami

International Cuban Sandwich Festival

Cinnamon Buttermilk Biscuits

2 cups self-rising flour
¼ cup sugar
1 teaspoon ground cinnamon
¼ teaspoon baking soda
⅓ cup Crisco shortening (not butter flavored)
½ cup raisins or currants, optional
¾ cup plus 2 tablespoons buttermilk

Preheat oven to 450°. In a large bowl, combine flour, sugar, cinnamon and baking soda; mix well. Cut in shortening with pastry blender or fork until mixture resembles coarse crumbs. Stir in raisins. Add ¾ cup buttermilk and mix well. Add 2 tablespoons buttermilk and continue to stir until mixture leaves sides of bowl and soft dough forms. Turn dough out onto floured surface; knead lightly until no longer sticky. Roll out dough to ½ inch thickness. Cut with floured biscuit cutter. Place on treated cookie sheet with sides touching. Bake 10 to 13 minutes or until light golden brown. Serve hot or cool on wire racks before serving. Delicious served with apricot jam.

International Cuban Sandwich Festival

Tampa • Last Weekend in March

The Cuban Sandwich Festival in Tampa will be taking place at Valencia College. This is a free family event with a dedicated area for kids. The festival will also be integrating art into the event, featuring many local talents. The mayor of Orlando has proclaimed February Cuban Sandwich Month; the mayors of Tampa and Miami have proclaimed March Cuban Sandwich Month. Come and watch as they attempt to make the biggest Cuban sandwich in the world. The goal is 130 feet, which would break the record currently held by Tampa. The sandwich will then be cut up and used to feed over 400 homeless people. Taste all the best Cuban sandwiches that Central Florida has to offer, and try out the past year's winners too.

813.407.6866 • www.iLOVECubanSandwiches.com
Facebook: Cuban Sandwich Festival

Sweet Potato Biscuits

1 large sweet potato, cooked and mashed (about ¾ cup)
⅓ cup milk
1½ cups all-purpose flour
2 tablespoons sugar
1 tablespoon baking powder
1 teaspoon salt
6 tablespoons cold butter, cut into pencil-eraser-size pieces

Combine sweet potato and milk in a bowl. In a separate large bowl, combine flour, sugar, baking powder and salt. Cut in butter with a knife or pastry blender. Pour in sweet potato-milk mixture a little bit at a time and mix well. Turn out onto a floured surface and knead dough lightly. Flatten with your hand or a rolling pin to ½ inch thick. Cut with a floured biscuit cutter and place each biscuit on a nonstick cookie sheet. Bake at 425° for 10 to 12 minutes or until golden brown.

Rebekah Chadwick

Florida Keys Seafood Festival

Marathon • Saturday and Sunday of Martin Luther King, Jr. Weekend

Featuring freshly caught Florida seafood including lobster, stone crabs, snapper, grouper, Key West pink shrimp and more. All locally and sustainably harvested, cleaned, cooked, and served by Florida Keys commercial fishermen and their families. Continuous live music both days, super raffles, and fun for the entire family.

6349 Overseas Highway Suite 4 • Marathon, FL 33050
813-362-9555 • www.floridakeysseafoodfestival.com
Facebook: flkeysseafoodfestival

Fried Biscuits with Honey-Butter Syrup

I always loved the fried biscuits served back in the day by mom-and-pop diners in Florida's Panhandle. I decided to try making them myself, and I think mine are actually better. They are best served hot straight from the skillet.

1 (16.3-ounce) can flaky biscuits
1 stick butter plus more for cooking
3 tablespoons syrup
2 tablespoons honey

Heat a cast-iron skillet or griddle. While skillet heats, separate biscuits in the middle so you have twice the number of biscuits. Place a little butter in the skillet and add a few biscuit halves. Brown on 1 side, flatten them a bit with your spatula, then flip and cook on the other side until both sides are a rich golden brown. While biscuits cook, melt 1 stick butter in a saucepan. Add syrup and honey and cook just long enough to melt butter and ingredients mix together (do not boil); remove from heat. Serve Fried Biscuits hot, drizzled with Honey-Butter Syrup.

Christine Morgan, Pensacola and Panama City

Key West Banana Pancakes

Country music star and songwriter Tim Charron splits his time between the Florida Keys and Nashville. Tim's brand of music is termed "country with a twist of lime." Here's his take on banana pancakes.

2 ripe bananas
3 eggs, beaten
½ cup ground flaxseed
½ tablespoon baking powder

Mash bananas in a bowl. Add eggs, flaxseed and baking powder; mix well. Chill in refrigerator 5 to 10 minutes. Heat a nonstick skillet over medium heat. Treat with nonstick spray. Pour ¼ cup pancake batter in skillet and cook until edges are browned and center just begins to firm. Wiggle your spatula under the pancake and gently flip. Cook until firm.

Tim Charron, Key West

German Oven Pancakes

We love these pancakes for Sunday breakfast. They are fast and easy to make.

- **3 tablespoons butter**
- **3 eggs, beaten until fluffy**
- **½ cup milk**
- **½ cup flour**
- **½ teaspoon salt**

Preheat oven to 450°. Put butter in an 8-inch pie plate; place in oven to melt. In a large bowl, combine eggs, milk, flour and salt; beat until smooth. Pour immediately into hot pie plate. Bake 18 minutes without opening oven door. Serve with butter, syrup or powdered sugar. Serves 2.

Sue Dannahower, Fort Pierce

Jalapeño & Salsa Breakfast Burritos

Breakfast burritos are one of my favorite dishes for starting a weekend day.

1 jalapeño pepper, divided
1 small white onion, sliced or chopped
1 green bell pepper, chopped
1 tablespoon oil or butter
4 large eggs, beaten
1 tablespoon milk
Salt and pepper
4 flour tortillas
1 cup shredded Mexican cheese blend
Salsa
Sour cream

Slice jalapeño in half lengthwise. Dice half; slice half and set aside. Sauté onion, green pepper and diced jalapeño in a frying pan with oil until soft. Combine eggs and milk; salt and pepper to taste. Add to skillet with vegetables; cook until eggs reach preferred firmness. Warm tortillas 10 seconds in microwave. Fill each with egg mixture, sprinkle with cheese and add a spoonful of salsa on top. Fold tortilla around egg mixture like an envelope. Serve on a plate with additional salsa, a spoonful of sour cream and reserved jalapeño slices.

Dani Hoy, Key West

Steak & Egg Breakfast Casserole

¾ pound thin-cut steak, cut into cubes
Salt and onion powder
2 tablespoons Everglades seasoning
¾ cup diced yellow onion
8 large eggs
2½ cups shredded Monterey Jack cheese, divided
2 teaspoon Italian seasoning
6 frozen biscuits, thawed
1 tablespoon parsley

Season steak with salt, onion powder and Everglades seasoning; cook with onion in a cast-iron skillet over medium heat until meat is medium well. Beat eggs and stir in 1 cup cheese and Italian seasoning. Treat a 3-quart casserole dish with nonstick spray. Press biscuits into bottom of dish; layer steak over biscuits. Pour egg mixture over steak and top with remaining cheese. Bake 20 minutes at 350°.

Jamie Martin, Newberry
Pampered Chef

Aunty Mame's Granola

This granola is over-the-top delicious.

    4 cups old-fashioned rolled oats
    1 (15-ounce) can cream of coconut
    ½ cup sugar-free juice (orange, berry, cranberry)
    ½ cup maple syrup or honey
    2 teaspoons garam masala
    1 cup chopped toasted nuts (pepitas, pecans, walnuts, sesame seeds, almonds)
    1 cup chopped dried fruit (prunes, dates, apples, berries, apricots)
    ¼ cup coconut flakes, optional

Preheat oven to 300°. In a mixing bowl, combine oats, cream of coconut, juice, maple syrup and garam marsala; blend well. Spread on a cookie tray. Bake 1 hour, tossing every 10 minutes until lightly crunchy and golden; cool. Mix baked oats with nuts and fruits. Refrigerate until ready to eat. Makes 12 (½ cup) servings (approximately 225 calories).

Alice Nash

Soups & Salads

Waterfront Boardwalk at Sunset, The Villages

Hamburger Soup

I served this wonderful soup often when my kids were growing up. It contains most of the food groups and freezes well. My family loves it served with cornbread.

2 pounds ground beef
¼ cup chopped onions
3 cups tomato juice
1 cup water
1 (1-ounce) package Lipton dry onion soup mix
2 (10.75-ounce) cans cream of celery soup
2 cups shredded carrots
4 stalks celery, sliced
¼ teaspoon pepper
¼ teaspoon marjoram
¼ teaspoon garlic salt
1 teaspoon sugar

In a Dutch oven, brown beef; drain. Add onion; brown. In a separate bowl, combine tomato juice, water, onion soup mix and cream of celery soup; stir until smooth. Add with remaining ingredients to beef mixture; simmer 30 minutes or until vegetables are tender. Serves 10.

Strawberry Fest of Clay County

Green Cove Springs • 1st Weekend in March

Come out for the Strawberry Fest, featuring family fun and festivities both inside and out. You'll enjoy delicious food, Plant City strawberries, arts and crafts, live entertainment, pony rides, a petting zoo, and so much more. Participate in the pie-eating contest, sack races, games, rock painting, and the hula hoop contest. You can also eat and drink the whole day, sampling treats like strawberry shortcake, chocolate-covered strawberries, strawberry lemonade, and so much more.

Clay County Fairgrounds • 2497 State Road 16 West
Green Cove Springs, FL 32043
386.860.0092 • www.claycountyfest.com
Facebook: ClayCountyStrawberryFest

Meaty, Feed-a-Cold Slow-Cooker Soup

We call this "snotty-nosed soup." Yes, that probably sounds gross, but this soup is perfect when you have a cold or are under the weather.

1 pound ground beef
Salt and pepper
1 (23-ounce) can vegetable beef soup
1 (10-ounce) can Rotel tomatoes, drained

1 (11-ounce) can niblets corn, drained
1 (10.75-ounce) can tomato soup
1 (15-ounce) can chili
Worcestershire sauce to taste
Hot sauce, optional

Brown and season ground beef. Add to slow cooker with remaining ingredients. Cook on low 4 to 6 hours. Serve hot with crackers, tortilla chips or toasted and buttered French bread slices.

Mary Farris, Pensacola and Panama City

Millie's Pasulj, aka Bean Soup

This bean soup from Serbia called "Pasulj" is the dish of love. My dad loved making this. While teaching me to make it, he would eat all the ham hocks as they were cooking. We would serve this with a loaf of hot homemade bread, chopped onions, and hot sauce.

½ pound dried white navy or great Northern beans, rinsed
1½ pounds ham hock or ham bone
Salt and pepper
3 carrots, peeled and sliced or medium chopped
3 medium red potatoes, peeled and cut into medium pieces

2 ribs celery, medium chopped
1 medium onion, medium chopped
1 clove garlic, finely chopped
4 tablespoons oil, optional
4 tablespoons all-purpose flour, optional
3 tablespoons sweet or hot paprika
Parsley for garnish

In a large soup pot, place beans, ham and 16 cups water. Bring to a boil. Stir occasionally so beans don't stick, and skim off any foam that rises to the surface. Add salt and pepper to taste. Lower temperature and simmer 1 hour. Add carrots, potatoes, celery, onion and garlic; return to a boil. Reduce heat and simmer 1 hour. Remove meat from ham bone and return to soup (discard bone). If soup isn't thick enough, add optional "zafrig" or thickener. In a small saucepan, add oil and flour and cook until light brown. Remove from heat and add paprika, stirring well. Return to low heat and add 1 cup bean soup, mixing well. Stir into soup pot and simmer 5 minutes or until soup is thickened to your liking. (If not using thickener, add paprika straight to pot.) Serve in heated bowls garnished with chopped parsley, if desired.

Millie Johnson, Melbourne

Ham & Black-Eyed Pea Soup

½ pound ham, cooked and cubed
2 (15-ounce) cans black-eyed peas, drained
4 cups chicken stock
1 onion, diced
3 carrots, peeled and diced
1 teaspoon dried sage
1 teaspoon dried thyme
1 teaspoon dried oregano
1½ cups frozen spinach, thawed
½ teaspoon crushed red pepper flakes
1 cup cooked rice

Combine ham, peas, chicken stock, onion, carrots, sage, thyme and oregano in a slow cooker. Add 3 cups water and give it all a stir. Cover and cook 4 to 5 hours on low. Stir in spinach and red pepper flakes; cook an additional 15 minutes. Stir in cooked rice before serving.

Jamie Martin, Newberry
Pampered Chef

Uncle Eric's Black Bean Soup

My uncle Eric Hernandez had a restaurant named Ruthie T's in Panama City, where he was also the chef. This homemade Black Bean Soup recipe comes from his personal collection and is made with chicken breast. It's wonderful and hearty.

3 to 4 chicken breasts	½ tablespoon cumin
2 (15-ounce) cans black beans, rinsed	½ tablespoon tarragon
2 bouillon cubes (chicken or beef)	½ tablespoon rosemary
1 large onion, diced	½ tablespoon marjoram
3 cloves garlic, finely diced	½ tablespoon basil
½ tablespoon coriander	3 to 4 bay leaves
½ tablespoon thyme	1 (8-ounce) package elbow macaroni

Simmer chicken breasts in a large pot in enough water to cover until tender. Remove chicken from water (reserving water), debone and remove any fat; set aside. Mash half the black beans. Add mashed and whole black beans along with remaining ingredients, except macaroni, to the water in the pot. Simmer 10 minutes. Add reserved chicken meat and macaroni; simmer 10 minutes or until macaroni is al dente. You may add additional water, or beer, depending on desired consistency. Serve hot and enjoy.

Lisa Barnes, Palm Beach

Creamy Cabbage & Kielbasa Soup

If you like cabbage, try this soup. It's creamy, savory, and the kielbasa adds a nice smoky flavor. This recipe makes a huge pot, but the leftovers taste even better.

2 tablespoons flour
1 cup chicken stock
1 medium head green cabbage, chopped
1½ pounds kielbasa, sliced in ⅛-inch rounds
1 large carrot, diced
2 (10.65-ounce) cans cream of celery soup
4 cups whole milk
1 cup heavy cream (or half-and-half)
¼ teaspoon dried thyme
¾ teaspoon salt
1 bay leaf
¼ teaspoon ground black pepper

Whisk flour into chicken stock until fully dissolved. Add stock and remaining ingredients to a Dutch oven or large soup pot. Bring to a boil. Reduce heat to medium and simmer, uncovered, 30 minutes, stirring occasionally.

Laurie Paddack Wilkes, Fort Myers

Kale & Kielbasa Soup

This recipe is a family favorite. The kale adds flavor and texture; it's our favorite part of the dish. It's perfect on a cool day. We usually double the recipe, and it's always better the next day after the flavors have time to blend.

- 1 pound smoked kielbasa, sliced
- 3 to 4 medium gold or red potatoes, chopped
- 1 large onion, chopped
- 2 tablespoons olive oil
- 1 to 2 bunches kale (or baby kale), trimmed and torn
- 4 cloves garlic, minced
- 1 (14.5-ounce) can diced tomatoes, undrained
- 1 (15-ounce) can garbanzo beans, rinsed and drained
- 4 cups chicken stock
- 1 teaspoon pepper
- 1 teaspoon salt
- 2 bay leaves

In a large pot or Dutch oven, cook sausage, potatoes and onion in oil 5 minutes over medium heat. Add kale, cover and cook 3 to 5 minutes until kale is wilted. (May have to add kale in parts to let it cook down before adding more.) Add garlic and cook 1 minute longer. Add remaining ingredients. Bring to a boil; reduce heat. Cover and simmer 9 to 12 minutes or until potatoes are tender. Discard bay leaves.

Bobby and Kimberly Earnhardt, originally from Jacksonville

One-Pot Fish Soup with Fennel & Thyme

1 tablespoon extra virgin olive oil
1 cup diced fennel stalks
1 cup diced carrot
1 cup diced onion
½ cup diced celery
2 cloves garlic, diced
4 cups fish, seafood, or chicken stock
1 tablespoon Himalayan or sea salt
1 teaspoon fresh ground pepper
2 to 3 fresh thyme sprigs
1 bay leaf
2 pounds grouper or cod fillets

Heat oil in a large pot, sauté fennel, carrot, onion and celery until semisoft. Add garlic and continue to sauté 1 minute. Add stock and 3 cups water. Season with salt and pepper; add thyme and bay leaf. Bring mixture to a rolling boil. Reduce heat and simmer at least 10 minutes. Add fish and simmer an additional 15 minutes. Fish should flake easily with a fork when done. Season with more salt and pepper to taste.

Tim and Vesna McGlen, Melbourne

Melbourne Beach

Crabby Potato Soup

4 large baking potatoes, washed and cubed (1-inch pieces)
1 Vidalia onion, chopped
½ tablespoon minced garlic
2 (14-ounce) cans chicken stock
2 tablespoons pepper
1 tablespoon salt
1 tablespoon Italian seasoning
1 teaspoon seafood seasoning
1 cup half-and-half
1 cup cooked lump crabmeat (if canned, drain)
2 cups shredded sharp Cheddar cheese (plus more for garnish)
Sour cream, for garnish
Finely chopped green onions for garnish
Bacon crumbles/bits for garnish

To a slow cooker, add potatoes, onion, garlic, stock and ¼ cup water. Season with pepper, salt, Italian seasoning and seafood seasoning. Cook on low 5 to 6 hours (or high 2 to 3 hours) or until potatoes are soft. When potatoes are done, mash with a fork or masher. Add half-and-half and cook an additional 30 minutes to an hour on high. Add crabmeat and 2 cups Cheddar cheese. Stir to warm crabmeat and melt cheese. Cover and keep warm until ready to serve. Thicken with a spoonful of flour or thin with milk, if desired. Serve topped with sour cream, green onions, additional cheese and bacon bits.

Tricia Benson Breast, Fleming Island

Valerie's French Onion Soup

3 tablespoons butter, melted
¼ cup oil
5 large yellow onions, sliced
3 large Spanish onions, sliced
6 cups beef stock
3 beef bouillon cubes
1 bay leaf
½ cup dry red wine
½ teaspoon salt
¼ teaspoon red pepper
⅛ teaspoon black pepper
Worcestershire sauce

Melt butter in a large saucepan; add oil. Sauté onions until soft, but not brown. Add beef stock, 3 cups water, bouillon cubes and bay leaf. Boil 15 minutes; reduce heat to low. Add wine, salt, red pepper and black pepper; simmer 1½ to 2 hours. Add Worcestershire to taste and mix well. Remove bay leaf and serve hot with cheesy French bread.

Jamie Martin, Newberry
Pampered Chef

Gazpacho

I love this cold vegetable soup. It is so healthy, utilizing fresh produce.

3 large tomatoes, peeled and finely chopped
1 green bell pepper, finely chopped
1 cucumber, peeled and finely chopped
1 cup finely chopped celery
½ cup finely chopped green onion
4 cups tomato juice
2 avocados, chopped
5 tablespoons red wine vinegar
4 tablespoons olive oil
2 teaspoons salt
1 clove garlic, crushed
½ teaspoon black pepper
Sour cream
Croutons

Combine all ingredients, except sour cream and croutons, in a large non-metallic bowl; chill overnight. Serve soup cold with a dollop of sour cream on top. Pass the croutons in a bowl. Serves 8.

Sue Dannahower, Fort Pierce

Corn & Crab Bisque

I make this soup for company. The bacon adds a wonderful salty-smoked flavor.

2 tablespoons butter
¼ cup flour
1 tablespoon olive oil
½ cup minced onion
1 cup uncooked corn (shucked from about 3 ears)
1 tablespoon minced garlic
2 tablespoons minced celery
1 cup clam stock
2 teaspoons salt
½ teaspoon white pepper
2 cups milk
2 cups heavy cream
1 teaspoon crab boil
½ pound lump crabmeat, picked
½ cup chopped green onions
4 slices bacon, cooked crisp and crumbled
½ teaspoon Worcestershire sauce

In a saucepan over medium heat, melt butter; whisk in flour 1 tablespoon at a time. Continue to cook, whisking constantly, until roux is thick and forms a ball, about 5 minutes. Set aside. In a large pot over high heat, heat olive oil; add onion and corn and sauté 1 minute. Stir in garlic and celery; sauté 30 seconds. Add stock, salt and pepper; bring to a boil. Stir in milk, cream and crab boil. Bring back to a boil; reduce heat to simmer, cook 5 to 7 minutes. Whisk in roux 1 tablespoon at a time. Reduce heat to low; whisk until mixture thickens. Stir in crabmeat, green onions, bacon and Worcestershire; simmer 6 to 8 minutes. Serve in cups and enjoy. Serves 6.

Sue Dannahower, Fort Pierce

Tomato Bisque

I made this bisque for "Home is Where the Art is," an ArtMundo fundraiser. It will warm your soul on a cold evening and excite your taste buds in the summer months. A good all seasons fill-you-up.

3 fresh cloves garlic, minced
1 onion, diced
1 tablespoon butter
2 (28-ounce) cans whole stewed tomatoes
2 (14-ounce) cans fire-roasted tomatoes
1 (29-ounce) can tomato sauce
Cooking sherry to taste
½ cup chopped fresh basil
Sea salt and pepper to taste
½ cup light cream cheese
Fresh Parmesan cheese, grated
Fresh parsley
Homemade croutons

In a Dutch oven over medium heat, sauté garlic and onion in butter until tender. Add tomatoes and tomato sauce; cook 10 minutes. Add sherry; cook an additional 10 minutes. Remove from heat; cool. Add basil, salt and pepper. Using a submersion blender or food processor, blend until smooth. Return to heat. Add cream cheese; stir to incorporate. Adjust seasoning to taste. Serve garnished with Parmesan, parsley and croutons. Serves 4 to 6.

Sue Dannahower, Fort Pierce

Oyster Stew

A delicious and hearty stew made with fresh oysters. A dash of hot sauce really sets off the flavor.

1 (12-ounce) container fresh oysters
2 tablespoons butter
½ medium onion, diced
2 tablespoons all-purpose flour
1 celery stalk, sliced

1½ cups whole milk
½ cup heavy cream
Salt and pepper to taste
Dash hot sauce, optional

Drain oysters reserving liquid. Rinse oysters well and chop if desired. Strain reserved liquid over fine mesh to remove any sediment. Melt butter in a saucepan over medium heat. Add onion and cook until golden. Stir in flour to coat. Add celery and oysters; cook 4 to 6 minutes or until oysters begin to curl around the edges. Add reserved oyster liquid, milk and cream; continue to cook until heated through. Add salt, pepper and hot sauce. Makes 4 (½-cup) servings.

Florida Dairy Farmers, Altamonte Springs

Apalachicola Oyster Cook-Off

Apalachicola • Friday and Saturday before Martin Luther King, Jr. Day

Welcome to the Oyster Cook-Off to benefit the Apalachicola Volunteer Fire Department. The event is held every year on Friday and Saturday before Martin Luther King, Jr. Day in downtown Historic Apalachicola at Riverfront Park. All proceeds go directly towards paying for the brand new fire truck they purchased a few years ago, due to this sole fundraising event. The event features a silent auction, oysters galore, shrimp, smoked mullet, hot dogs, hamburgers, local beer, live music, kids' activities, dancing performances and a 5K run.

180 4th Street • Apalachicola, FL 32320
850.323.0385 • www.oystercookoff.com
Facebook: oystercookoff

Uncle Charles' Oyster Chowder Stew

Uncle Charles grew up on the Gulf Coast, spending much of his time at his family's house located in Saint Teresa, Florida. Charles is a great cook and often lends his talents to cooking in large quantities for charity events and to participating in chili cook-offs. This recipe is for a very hearty Oyster Chowder Stew.

—Kent Whitaker

 2 large white potatoes, sliced
 5 sticks butter
 2 stalks celery, chopped
 ½ cup chopped onion
 1 tablespoon flour
 1½ to 2 quarts milk
 ½ teaspoon salt
 ½ teaspoon white or black pepper
 ½ teaspoon Old Bay seafood seasoning
 Tabasco or Worcestershire sauce to taste
 1 quart oysters plus oyster liquor

Boil potatoes in salted water to cover until tender; drain. Melt butter in a Dutch oven or large pot over medium heat. Sauté celery and onion until tender. Add flour and stir. Whisk in milk. Add potatoes, salt, pepper, seafood seasoning and Tabasco. Add oysters and oyster liquor. Simmer over medium heat about 5 minutes to allow flavors to blend. Adjust seasoning if needed. Serve hot with oyster or saltine crackers.

Charles Johnson, Tallahassee

Homemade Beef Stew

2 pounds beef stew meat
2 tablespoons whole-wheat flour
Kosher salt and freshly ground pepper to taste
3 tablespoons olive oil, divided
4 cups low-sodium vegetable stock, divided
1 medium Florida onion, chopped
2 medium Florida tomatoes, diced
1 tablespoon fresh Florida thyme leaves, or 2 teaspoons dried
6 Florida carrots, peeled, halved lengthwise, cut into 1-inch pieces
3 medium Florida potatoes, peeled and cut into 1-inch cubes
¼ cup minced Florida parsley leaves

Cut stew meat into 1½-inch cubes and pat dry. In large bowl, toss beef cubes with flour, salt and pepper. Warm 1 tablespoon oil in large, heavy saucepan. Add half the meat in a single layer without crowding pan. Brown on all sides, about 5 to 7 minutes. Remove beef and transfer to bowl. Add ¼ cup stock to pot and stir with a wooden spoon, scraping loose any browned bits on the bottom of the pan. Transfer to bowl with meat. Repeat cooking procedure with another 1 tablespoon oil and remaining meat. Add remaining 1 tablespoon oil to pot over medium-low heat. Add onion and cook 5 minutes, stirring occasionally. Return reserved beef and juices to pan. Add remaining stock, tomatoes and thyme. If necessary, add water to cover. Increase heat and bring to a boil. Reduce heat to medium low, cover and simmer 1 hour. Add carrots and potatoes to pan. Let simmer, covered, 45 minutes or until beef is very tender and vegetables are cooked through. Add water, if needed, to bring stew to desired consistency. Serve hot with biscuits and garnish with parsley.

www.freshfromflorida.com

Fall Harvest Chowder

1 teaspoon olive oil
1 cup chopped Florida onion
1½ tablespoons chopped fresh garlic
2 stalks Florida celery, sliced
1 cup sliced Florida carrots
1 cup fresh Florida corn kernels
2 cups cubed Florida potatoes
2 teaspoons cooking sherry (or white wine)
1 bay leaf
1 tablespoon chopped fresh Florida thyme (or 1 teaspoon dried)
1 tablespoon chopped fresh Florida marjoram (or 1 teaspoon dried)
1 tablespoon chopped fresh Florida rosemary (or 1 teaspoon dried)
2 cups low-sodium vegetable stock
Cayenne to taste
Kosher salt and freshly ground pepper to taste
1 bunch green onion, sliced small

Heat oil in a large heavy saucepan. Add onion and sauté 5 minutes. Add garlic, celery, carrots, corn, potatoes, sherry, bay leaf and herbs. Stir in vegetable stock and cover. Bring to boil and cook over medium heat 10 to 15 minutes, or until potatoes and corn are tender. Discard bay leaf. Purée 1 cup soup in blender and return to pot. Season with cayenne, salt and pepper. Garnish with green onion when serving.

TIP: Add shredded chicken to turn this recipe into a complete meal. Also try garnishing with sour cream seasoned with salt and pepper.

www.freshfromflorida.com

All-American Potato Salad

4 pounds large red potatoes
½ cup cider vinegar
3 tablespoons vegetable oil
1½ teaspoons salt
¾ teaspoon freshly ground pepper
1½ cups mayonnaise
3 tablespoons Dijon mustard
1 celery stalk, finely chopped (optional)
½ cup finely chopped red onion
8 slices bacon, cooked and crumbled
4 eggs, boiled, peeled and quartered

Clean potatoes well; leave the skin on. In a large pot, cover potatoes with salted water. Bring to a boil; reduce heat to medium and cook 25 to 30 minutes or until potatoes are tender when pierced with a sharp knife. Drain and set aside to cool. While potatoes cool, whisk vinegar, oil, salt and pepper in a large bowl until blended. When potatoes are cool enough to handle but still warm, cut into ¾-inch chunks (you may peel them at this point but the salad is great with skin on). Add warm potatoes to vinegar mixture; gently stir to coat. Set aside. In a small bowl, whisk mayonnaise and mustard until blended; pour over potatoes and stir. Add celery and onion; stir gently to mix. Serve immediately topped with crumbled bacon and egg quarters. (If you prefer cold potato salad; refrigerate before topping with bacon and eggs when ready to serve.)

Cornbread Salad

1 large pan cooked cornbread, crumbled (1 9x13-inch pan or 2 10-inch iron skillets)
1½ cups mayonnaise
1 cup celery, finely chopped
1 green pepper, seeded and chopped
¾ cup green onions, chopped
1 (5-ounce) jar green olives with pimentos, drained and chopped
2 large tomatoes, chopped
1 teaspoon sage
Salt and pepper to taste
10 slices bacon, fried and crumbled
1 (4.5-ounce) can chopped green chiles, drained

Combine all ingredients in a large bowl; mix well. Refrigerate 3 to 4 hours before serving.

The Heintz & Becker De Soto Seafood Festival

Palmetto • Last Weekend in March

The Heintz & Becker De Soto Seafood Festival is widely recognized as one of Florida's most outstanding events and attended by thousands each year. A great lineup of continuous entertainment includes the best the local music scene has to offer as well as nationally-known recording artists.

Sutton & Lamb Parks • 6th Street West and 10th Avenue West
Palmetto, FL 34221
941.747.1998

Cubano Black Bean & Crab Salad

This recipe is a side salad, but I also serve it as a dip, on occasion, with tortilla chips. Use fresh cooked and chilled crabmeat if you can. If not, use as fresh as you can get when inland or even imitation crabmeat. I split my time between Florida and Chattanooga, Tennessee, with my business Scenic City Yachts. I love the Cuban flavors of Miami reflected in this dish.

2 (15-ounce) cans black beans, drained
1 small tomato, chopped
1 jalapeño pepper, finely chopped
1½ tablespoons lime juice
2 teaspoons olive oil
1 teaspoon chopped cilantro
2 green onions, finely chopped
2 tablespoons finely chopped green bell pepper
1 cup whole-kernel corn
Salt and pepper to taste
1 cup cooked, chilled and crumbled fancy lump crabmeat
Tortilla chips for garnish

Combine all ingredients, except crabmeat and chips. Stir to mix evenly, cover and chill at least an hour. Taste and add additional seasonings if needed. Stir in crabmeat just before serving; garnish with chips if desired.

Garrett Gamble, Key West
Scenic City Yachts

Black Bean & Corn Salad

4 ears corn, husks removed
2 tablespoons oil
1 cup diced red bell pepper
¾ cup diced red onion
¼ cup cider vinegar
1 (15-ounce) can black beans, rinsed and drained
1 teaspoon minced garlic
½ cup julienned snow peas
1 teaspoon each salt and pepper

Preheat oven to broil. Place corn (on cob) in oven and broil about 3 minutes per side or until slightly brown. Cut kernels from cob using a serrated knife; set aside. Heat oil in a medium sauté pan over medium-high heat. Add bell pepper and onion; sauté 3 minutes. Add vinegar, beans and corn. Sauté 2 minutes. Stir in garlic and snow peas; sauté 1 minute longer. Remove from heat to a serving bowl and season with salt and pepper. Serve warm or cold. Serves 6.

Grant Seafood Festival

Grant • March

Grant Seafood Festival is the southeastern United States' longest running seafood festival, celebrating for over fifty years. The festival is run on 100% volunteer effort, proceeds going towards a scholarship fund. The festival does not have food vendors but rather community volunteers, oftentimes several generations, all working together to serve up menu items that have been passed down throughout the years. Come enjoy live entertainment and more than 100 crafters. Parking and admission are free.

4580 1st Street • Grant, FL 32949
321.723.8687 • www.grantseafoodfestival.com
Facebook:grantseafoodfestival

Easy Vegan Three-Bean Salad

Fresh summer produce gave me the idea for this Easy Vegan Three-Bean Salad. It's perfect for cookouts, beach days or a quiet day at home.

12 ounces fresh green beans
1 pint cherry or grape tomatoes, halved or quartered
1 (15-ounce) can garbanzo beans, drained and rinsed
12 ounces shelled edamame
2 green onions, sliced
¼ cup diced red onion, optional
½ teaspoon coarse ground sea salt
¼ teaspoon fresh ground pepper
2 to 3 tablespoons extra virgin olive oil
1 tablespoon fresh lemon juice

Steam green beans until crisp-tender, about 10 minutes. Remove from steamer and run under cold water; drain and cut into bite-size pieces. Mix with remaining ingredients in a large bowl. Toss well.

Dawn Hutchins, St. Johns
Florida Coastal Cooking & Wellness

Grant Seafood Festival

Charron Chicken Salad

This is a very simple recipe. It's all about the rosemary.

- **1 whole chicken**
- **2 tablespoons olive oil**
- **4 to 5 small sprigs fresh rosemary**
- **½ cup mayonnaise**
- **Salt and pepper to taste**
- **2 to 3 teaspoon fresh dill or to taste**

Rub chicken with olive oil. Bake in a preheated oven at 325° for 1 hour. Top with 2 to 3 fresh rosemary sprigs, securing with a toothpick if needed. Place 1 to 2 sprigs inside the chicken cavity. Continue cooking another 20 to 30 minutes or until juice runs clear and chicken is completely done; cool. Shred breast meat into a bowl. Mix with mayonnaise, salt, pepper and dill.

Tim Charron, Key West

Waldorf Chicken Salad with Honey-Lemon Sauce

- **2 to 3 boneless, skinless chicken breasts, cooked and cubed**
- **¼ cup mayonnaise**
- **¼ cup sour cream**
- **1 tablespoon freshly squeezed lemon juice**
- **1 medium sweet apple, cored and diced**
- **½ cup red seedless grapes, halved**
- **½ cup thinly sliced celery**
- **½ cup chopped toasted walnuts**
- **Salt and pepper to taste**

Combine everything in a bowl and gently fold to mix. Chill before serving. This chunky version is perfect served atop lettuce or mixed salad greens. Chop everything a bit finer to serve with fancy crackers or even as mini party sandwiches.

Denise Johnson, Melbourne

Three-Step Salad with Homemade Ranch Dressing

This recipe combines a simple salad with a terrific homemade ranch dressing.

Salad:

Step 1: Buy a bag of mixed salad greens. Rinse and set aside to drain.

Step Two: Add in something sweet and something salty. Sweet can be dried cranberries, Mandarin orange slices or anything else you enjoy. Salty suggestions include sunflower seeds, croutons, packaged salad toppings or walnuts.

Step 3: Add meat—grilled chicken pieces, leftover steak slices, pepperoni or shrimp.

Homemade Ranch Dressing:

⅓ cup buttermilk
3 to 4 tablespoons sour cream
3 to 4 tablespoons mayonnaise
1 teaspoon lemon juice
½ tablespoon minced garlic
¼ teaspoon salt
1 tablespoon minced red bell pepper
2 green onions, minced
2 teaspoons parsley flakes
½ teaspoon minced cilantro
Black pepper to taste

Use fresh ingredients for the herbs and garlic if possible, but store-bought, dried herbs will work as well. Combine all ingredients in a blender or food processor and gently pulse. Add additional milk to thin or sour cream to thicken, if needed.

Christine Morgan, Pensacola and Panama City

Mixed Berry Salad with White Gold Peach Wine Dressing

The dressing makes this salad special. I sometimes use our Florida Orange Groves Winery's Mango Mammo wine instead of White Gold Peach. Both are delicious, and the dressing works just as well as a dip for fruit. Simply add more sour cream to thicken.

½ cup fat-free mayonnaise
¼ cup fat-free sour cream
¼ cup milk
3 tablespoons White Gold peach wine
1 (10-ounce) package mixed salad greens
2½ cups sliced fresh peaches
1 cup fresh blueberries
1 cup quartered fresh strawberries
½ cup sliced almonds, toasted if desired

For the dressing, whip together mayonnaise, sour cream, milk and wine. Cover and refrigerate while preparing salad. Wash and drain salad greens. Place on chilled salad plates. Arrange fruit on top of greens and sprinkle with almonds. Drizzle dressing over salad.

Lance Shook, St. Petersburg
Florida Orange Groves Winery

5-Minute Mandarin Orange–Spring Mix Salad

6 cups spring mix lettuce
½ medium red onion, thin sliced
1 (11-ounce) can Mandarin oranges, drained
1 cup sweetened dried cranberries
1 cup sliced almonds
1¼ cups crumbled feta cheese
1 cup strawberry balsamic vinaigrette salad dressing
½ cup McCormick salad topping

Combine lettuce, onion and oranges in a bowl; toss gently. Add cranberries, almonds, and feta cheese. Toss gently again. When ready to serve, top with dressing and salad topping.

Michael Whitfield, Jacksonville

Barberville Strawberry Fest

Barberville • 3rd Weekend in March

Have a strawberry-licious time with family fun and festivities inside and out including a Berry Cute Baby Contest and live entertainment. You'll enjoy delicious food including many yummy strawberry treats—strawberry fudge, strawberry ice cream, strawberry lemonade—plus plenty of Plant City strawberries. This family-friendly event also offers lots of fun for the kids including bounce houses, petting farm, pony ride, sack races, face painting, train rides, and much more.

1776 Lightfoot Lane • Barberville, FL 32105
386.860.0092 • www.barbervillefest.com
Facebook: BarbervilleStrawberryFest

Beet & Fried Goat Cheese Salad

1 (16-ounce) bag mixed greens
   (baby kale, baby spinach, arugula, romaine lettuce)
3 fresh small beets, sliced
4 ounces goat cheese, chunked and fried
1 red onion, sliced and caramelized
2 Granny Smith apples, thinly sliced
Top with your favorite vinaigrette dressing

In a large bowl, add greens; layer beets, goat cheese, onion and apples on top. When you get ready to serve, serve with your favorite vinaigrette dressing

Sally Kees, Fernandina Beach

Tropical Mango, Macadamia & Chèvre Salad

I love sharing good food with family and friends. Since opening my business, Personal Chef Tampa Bay, in 1995, I've had the opportunity to study culinary arts around the world: from Johnson and Wales in Singapore, to the Culinary Institute of America in Napa Valley, to China, Japan, Italy, France, Germany, and more. I'm passionate about all foods from vegan to game meats, organic to decadence and Parisian to down-home country cooking.

2 mangoes, divided
¼ cup vinegar (cider or balsamic)
1 tablespoon olive oil
½ teaspoon salt
¼ teaspoon freshly ground black pepper
1 teaspoon Dijon mustard
1 teaspoon minced shallot
8 cups spring greens
2 ounces honey chèvre (goat cheese), cut ½ inch thick
2 ounces macadamia nuts, crushed

Peel 1 mango and chop. Process in a food processor with vinegar, oil, salt, pepper, Dijon and shallot until smooth. Chill before using. When ready to serve, peel and dice remaining mango. Divide salad greens between 8 plates. Top each with diced mango, chèvre and nuts. Drizzle with chilled dressing.

Chef Eileen Morris, Crystal Beach
www.personalcheftampabay.com

Creamy Homemade Ranch Dressing

This very easy recipe is great on a salad but also works for a vegetable dip and even as a sauce for hamburgers, fried shrimp, French fries…almost anything. It's best when made a day or two ahead for better flavor. You can even use low-fat items, if you wish—even low-fat milk instead of buttermilk. There's a flavor difference but it's still good.

- ½ cup mayonnaise
- ½ cup sour cream
- ¼ cup buttermilk
- ½ teaspoon dried parsley
- ½ teaspoon dried dill
- ½ teaspoon dried chives
- Salt and pepper to taste

Combine everything in a bowl and mix well. Store in an airtight container in the refrigerator. (I use a glass canning jar.)

Jeff Collins, Hollywood

Thai Coconut Tahini Dressing

Here's a simple salad dressing recipe that includes it all. It's creamy, nutty and just a little tangy with coconut, tahini, and fresh lime. To make a good dressing, you need a fat, an acid, and a salt. They're the tin man, scarecrow, and cowardly lion of your dressing. You must have them all or you're not getting to Kansas.

1 (14.5-ounce) can coconut milk
⅓ cup tahini
¼ teaspoon Himalayan pink salt
Juice of 1 lime
1 Thai pepper, optional

Blend all ingredients in a blender until smooth.

Dawn Hutchins, St. Johns
Florida Coastal Cooking & Wellness

Pensacola Seafood Festival

Pensacola • Last Weekend in September

Savor delicious seafood, enjoy various musical acts, and immerse yourself in historic downtown Pensacola. The Pensacola Seafood Festival is one of the largest arts and crafts fairs in northwest Florida, with more than 170 artisans and craftsmen who travel from around the country to participate.

Downtown Pensacola • Pensacola, FL 32502
850.433.6512 • www.pensacolaseafoodfestival.com
Facebook: fiestapensacola

Lisa's Favorite Coleslaw

This recipe is one of my favorite recipes of all time. Not just because it's so simple, but because it connects so many wonderful memories for me. When Granddad would say "Who wants seafood?" Nana would make her signature salmon patties and hushpuppies and would suggest I make a batch of my coleslaw. A simple recipe with so many wonderful memories.

½ head fresh cabbage
1 carrot, peeled
1 teaspoon sugar
½ teaspoon salt
Mayonnaise to taste

Using a grater, shred cabbage and carrot into a bowl. Season with the sugar and salt and toss. Add mayonnaise, 2 tablespoons at a time, while mixing until salad is your desired consistency. Chill at least 1 hour or until ready to serve. Every batch needs a different amount of mayonnaise depending on the size of the cabbage. I suggest making it light on mayonnaise then adjusting the mayo and seasonings after chilling, if needed.

Lisa Barnes, Palm Beach

Florida Blueberry Festival

Blueberry Jell-O Salad

This recipe is a family favorite from my grandmother. She wanted everyone to know it came from a recipe from her mom's recipe collection, my great grandmother, Joyce Ball. So, it's now a family tradition across four generations. We hope you enjoy it.

1 (6-ounce) box black cherry Jell-O
1 (15-ounce) can blueberries in heavy syrup
1 (20-ounce) can crushed pineapple, drained
1 (8-ounce) package cream cheese, softened
1 cup sour cream
½ cup sugar
1 teaspoon vanilla extract
1 cup chopped pecans

Dissolve Jell-O in 2 cups boiling water; add blueberries and pineapple. Gently pour into a glass baking dish and place in the refrigerator until set. When ready to serve, combine cream cheese, sour cream, sugar and vanilla with an electric mixer. Spread over salad and sprinkle pecans on top. Refrigerate leftovers.

Jared Ball for his grandmother Virginia Ball, Orlando

Florida Blueberry Festival

Kissimmee • March

The Florida Blueberry Festival is a four-day event featuring free music on the amphitheater grounds of the Formosa Gardens Event Center. Enjoy a wine garden in the Island Grove Wine Company Formosa Gardens or tour the Beer Garden for both craft and domestic choices. Sample twenty different vendors at the Festival Fare Food Court, then shop fine arts and crafts, fresh blueberry baked goods, and more. There is also a kids zone with inflatables, bungee jumping, rock climbing, and other fun activities for kids of all ages.

3050 Formosa Gardens Boulevard
Kissimmee, FL 34747
407.507.0015 • Facebook: FloridaBlueberryFestival

Strawberry Pretzel Salad

2 cups crushed pretzel sticks
¾ cup plus 4 tablespoons sugar, divided
¾ cup melted butter
1 (8-ounce) package cream cheese, softened
1 (8-ounce) container Cool Whip
1 (6-ounce) package strawberry Jell-O
2 (10-ounce) packages frozen strawberries, slightly thawed

In a bowl, combine pretzels, 4 tablespoons sugar and butter; spread in a 9x13-inch pan. Bake at 400° for 6 to 10 minutes; cool thoroughly. Mix cream cheese, Cool Whip and ¾ cup sugar; pour over crust. Dissolve Jell-O in 2 cups boiling water; add strawberries. Chill until almost congealed; spread over cream cheese mixture. Chill until completely set. Can be served as a salad or dessert. Best if made the night before.

Pam Whittle, Bradford County Strawberry Festival

Vegetables & Other Side Dishes

Cape Florida Lighthouse

Chris's Cuban Black Beans

My Cuban Black Beans have a bit of added flavor from beer. I prefer to use a local craft beer, so choose your favorite and enjoy.

1 tablespoon olive oil
2 cloves garlic, minced
1 cup chopped onion
½ bell pepper, chopped
1 (30-ounce) can black beans, rinsed
4 to 6 ounces beer
¼ cup chopped fresh cilantro (½ tablespoons dried)
½ teaspoon salt
1 to 2 teaspoons black pepper
Badia Complete Seasoning (Cuban spice blend)

Add olive oil to a large saucepan over medium heat. Add garlic and onion and sauté until aromatic. Add bell pepper and sauté until soft. Add black beans, beer, cilantro, salt, pepper and Cuban seasoning to taste. Continue to cook until heated through. Serve hot.

Key West Chris, aka Chris Rehm
Key West musician and songwriter

Calico Beans

I obtained this recipe from a Boy Scout potluck. It has been a party hit ever since.

½ (16-ounce) package bacon, chopped
1 onion, chopped
1 pound ground beef
1 (15-ounce) can pork 'n' beans
1 (15-ounce) can kidney beans
1 (15-ounce) can garbanzo beans
1 (15-ounce) can great Northern beans
½ cup barbecue sauce
¼ cup packed brown sugar
2 tablespoons mustard

In a large saucepan, brown bacon, onion and beef. Drain. Combine the rest of the ingredients with beef mixture. Pour into a 9x13-inch baking dish; bake at 350° for 1 hour. Serves 10 to 12.

Sue Dannahower, Fort Pierce

Jen Jo's Daytona Pinto Beans

Jen Jo Cobb is a team owner and driver in both the NASCAR Camping World Truck Series and the ARCA Racing Series. She's also the team cook most of the time. Here's one of her recipes that she serves up at Daytona International Speedway and Homestead.

2 (15-ounce) cans pinto beans, rinsed and drained
1 cup taco sauce (not salsa)
⅓ (16-ounce) package Velveeta cheese, cubed

Combine all ingredients in a saucepan over medium heat. Cook until small bubbles appear then turn down to simmer. (Do not allow it to boil.) You can easily add another can of beans if you need to feed additional people—which is often the case during a race weekend.

Jen Jo Cobb, Jennifer Jo Cobb Racing, LLC

Family Salsa Festival

Wimauma • March

The Family Salsa Festival is Wimauma's signature fundraising event, held each March. The festival is a celebration of the community and all things salsa. Come join in and sample the cuisine offered by various food vendors. Move your toes or your whole body to entertainment with a Latin beat. There are also lots of games and activities for the whole family. Shop at craft vendors and learn about local businesses and nonprofit organizations.

14920 Balm Wimauma Road • Wimauma, FL 33598
813.634.7136 • www.gsmission.org
Facebook: GoodSamMissionWimauma

Smothered Bacon–Green Bean Casserole

4 (15-ounce) cans green beans
2 tablespoons soy sauce
⅓ cup packed light brown sugar
¼ cup melted butter
1 teaspoon garlic powder
¼ teaspoon salt
¼ teaspoons pepper
10 slices bacon, cooked and chopped

Preheat oven to 350°. Drain and rinse green beans and pour into a large mixing bowl; set aside. In a smaller bowl, combine soy sauce, sugar, butter, garlic powder, salt and pepper; stir well. Pour over green beans; add bacon. Gently stir until evenly coated. Pour into a 9x13-inch casserole dish or baking pan. Bake uncovered 30 minutes.

Steinhatchee Fiddler Crab Festival, Steinhatchee

Indian Corn Casserole

This Thanksgiving Day favorite for my family is very easy to make and only takes a few ingredients.

1 (10.75-ounce) can whole-kernel corn, undrained
1 (10.75-ounce) can cream-style corn
1 (8.5-ounce) package Jiffy cornmeal muffin mix
1 cup sour cream
1 cup grated mozzarella cheese
1 stick butter, melted

Combine corn, muffin mix and sour cream; pour into greased 9x13-inch pan. Combine cheese and butter; mix well. Spoon evenly over cornbread mixture. Bake in a preheated 350° oven 1 hour.

Cindy Walker, Lakeland

Floral City Strawberry Festival

Floral City • 1st Weekend in March

The Floral City Strawberry Festival is an annual favorite in Citrus County as we celebrate spring and all things strawberry. The hundreds upon hundreds of strawberry flats are provided by Ferris Farms, a local grower that resides just a few miles away from the festival grounds.

9530 South Parkside Avenue • Floral City, FL 34436
352.795.3149 • www.gostrawberryfest.com
Facebook: FloralCityStrawberryFestival

Succotash

1 (16-ounce) package frozen butter beans
1 (16-ounce) package frozen shoepeg corn
6 slices bacon, chopped
2 cups sliced okra
1 stick butter, divided
½ teaspoon hot sauce
1 teaspoon chicken base
4 tomatoes, diced

In a stockpot over medium heat, place butter beans and corn with salted water to cover. Cook until beans are tender, about 30 minutes. In a deep skillet, sauté bacon until rendered but not crunchy. Drain corn and butter beans reserving ½ cup cooking liquid; add vegetables and reserved liquid to skillet. Add okra, 4 tablespoons butter, hot sauce and chicken base; cover and simmer 15 minutes. Stir in tomatoes and remaining butter; cook just until butter is melted and tomatoes are hot. Serve immediately.

Shoepeg Casserole

1 large onion, chopped
1 large green pepper, chopped
2 tablespoons plus 1 stick butter, divided
3 (11-ounce) cans shoepeg corn, drained
2 (15-ounce) cans French-style green beans, drained and chopped slightly
1 (10.75-ounce) can cream of celery soup
1 (10.75-ounce) can chicken soup
1 sleeve Ritz crackers

In a skillet over medium heat, sauté onion and green pepper in two tablespoons butter until soft. In a 9x13-inch dish, combine sautéed vegetables with corn, green beans and both soups; mix well and smooth top. Crush crackers and spread on top. Melt stick butter and drizzle over crackers. Bake at 350° for 30 minutes.

Zucchini & Corn Casserole

1½ pounds zucchini, chopped
1 (8-ounce) can cream-style corn
2 eggs, lightly beaten
1 cup chopped Vidalia onion
½ cup chopped red bell pepper
4 tablespoons butter
½ teaspoon salt
¼ teaspoon black pepper
1 teaspoon paprika
2 tablespoons cream cheese
1 cup grated sharp Cheddar cheese

Preheat oven to 350°. In a saucepan over medium heat, bring salted water to a boil. Add zucchini and cook about 5 minutes or until barely tender (do not overcook); drain. Add corn and eggs; mix. Sauté onion and bell pepper in butter until golden brown, about 5 minutes. Add to zucchini and corn mixture and season with salt, pepper and paprika. Add cream cheese and mix. Pour into a treated 3-quart casserole dish. Cover with Cheddar cheese. Bake, uncovered, 25 minutes, or until lightly browned and bubbly.

Zucchini Fries

2 zucchini
½ cup all-purpose flour
Kosher salt
Fresh ground black pepper
2 eggs
½ cup panko breadcrumbs
¼ cup grated Parmesan cheese
½ teaspoon smoked paprika

Preheat oven to 425°. Slice zucchini into ½-inch-thick and 4-inch-long "fries." Place flour in a shallow dish and season to taste with salt and pepper. Beat eggs in separate shallow dish. In a third dish, mix breadcrumbs, Parmesan and paprika; add salt and pepper to taste. Dip zucchini in flour, then in egg; roll in breadcrumb mixture. Place on a treated baking sheet. Bake 20 minutes flipping halfway through cook time.

Sautéed Zucchini

1 tablespoon olive oil
1 red onion, thinly sliced
3 cloves garlic, minced
4 medium zucchinis, sliced
1 (8-ounce) can tomato sauce

Heat olive oil in a large skillet over medium-high heat. Add onion and garlic; sauté 3 to 4 minutes or until onion is tender. Add zucchini and cook 4 minutes. Stir in tomato sauce and cook until zucchini is tender. Serves 4.

Spinach-Stuffed Squash

5 large yellow squash, halved
2 tablespoons olive oil
¾ teaspoon salt
¼ teaspoon ground black pepper
1 (10-ounce) package frozen chopped spinach, thawed
2 tablespoons butter
½ cup diced onion
1 cup chicken-flavored stuffing mix
½ cup sour cream
1 cup shredded sharp Cheddar cheese

Preheat oven to 400°. Brush cut side of squash with olive oil; sprinkle with salt and pepper. Place on a treated baking sheet, cut side down. Bake 15 minutes or until tender. Scoop out pulp, keeping shells intact; reserve pulp. Squeeze spinach dry and set aside. Reduce oven to 350°. In a large skillet, melt butter over medium heat. Add onion; cook 5 minutes or until transparent. Add stuffing mix, spinach, sour cream, cheese and reserved squash pulp. Mix well and season to taste with salt and pepper. Cook 3 more minutes. Spoon into squash shells on baking sheet; bake about 20 minutes.

Baked Parmesan Potato Wedges

4 large baking potatoes
4 teaspoons olive oil
½ cup grated Parmesan cheese
2 teaspoons Italian seasoning
Salt to taste
2 teaspoons garlic powder
2 teaspoons paprika
Mustard for dipping

Preheat oven to 400°. Wash potatoes; cut into wedges. Place wedges in a bowl; coat evenly with olive oil. In another bowl, mix Parmesan, Italian seasoning, salt, garlic powder and paprika; pour over wedges and mix until well coated. Line a baking pan with foil; place wedges flat without touching. Bake 40 minutes. Serve with mustard.

Steinhatchee Fiddler Crab Festival, Steinhatchee

Creamy Potato Sticks

¼ cup all-purpose flour
½ teaspoon salt
1½ cups milk
1 (10.75-ounce) can cream of celery soup
1 cup shredded Cheddar cheese
5 to 6 baking potatoes, peeled
1 cup chopped onion

Preheat oven to 350°. In a saucepan over medium heat, combine flour and salt; gradually whisk in milk until smooth. Bring to a boil; cook and stir 2 minutes. Remove from heat. Whisk in soup and cheese until smooth. Set aside. Cut potatoes into ½-inch sticks; place in a greased 9x13-inch baking dish. Sprinkle with onion. Top with cheese sauce. Bake uncovered 55 to 60 minutes or until potatoes are tender. Serves 6.

Easy Potato Puffs

1½ cups leftover mashed potatoes
1 egg, separated
¼ cup milk
3 tablespoons melted butter

Preheat oven to 350°. Beat potatoes, egg yolk, milk and butter until light; set aside. Beat egg white until stiff peaks form. Stir into potatoes. Drop by spoonfuls onto a greased baking sheet. Bake 15 minutes or until golden brown.

Sunshine Sweet Potatoes

Streusel Topping:
1 cup all-purpose flour
⅔ cup packed brown sugar
¼ cup chopped Florida pecans, toasted
¼ cup margarine, melted
½ teaspoon ground cinnamon

Potatoes:
2 pounds sweet potatoes, peeled and cut into 1-inch cubes
⅓ cup Florida honey
¼ cup Florida orange juice
1 tablespoon grated Florida orange zest
1 tablespoon grated lemon zest
½ teaspoon ground nutmeg
¼ teaspoon kosher salt, or to taste
⅛ teaspoon white pepper

Combine Streusel Topping ingredients in a small bowl, stirring to form a streusel. Set aside. Place sweet potatoes in a large saucepan with water to cover. Bring to a boil over high heat. Reduce heat to medium, cover and cook until tender, about 10 minutes. Drain sweet potatoes and cool. Preheat oven to 350°. Transfer sweet potatoes to a large bowl. Using a potato masher or a fork, mash sweet potatoes until smooth. In a small saucepan, combine honey, orange juice, orange zest, lemon zest, nutmeg, salt and pepper. Bring mixture to a boil over medium heat, stirring to melt honey. Stir into sweet potatoes. Spoon sweet potatoes into a 1-quart casserole and smooth down top. Sprinkle streusel mixture evenly over casserole. Bake until heated through, about 20 to 25 minutes.

www.freshfromflorida.com

Sweet Potato Balls

4 large sweet potatoes, baked
⅔ cup packed brown sugar
½ teaspoon ground nutmeg
1 orange
2 cups shredded coconut
½ cup sugar
1 teaspoon ground cinnamon
1 (10-ounce) bag miniature marshmallows

Preheat oven to 350°. Peel and mash sweet potatoes with brown sugar and nutmeg. Zest orange adding 2 teaspoons to potatoes. Juice orange adding 2 tablespoons; mix well. In a separate bowl, toss coconut with sugar and cinnamon. Place 1 marshmallow on top of sweet potatoes; cover with sweet potatoes forming a 2-inch ball. Roll in coconut and place on a treated baking pan. Repeat using all sweet potato mixture. Bake 15 to 20 minutes.

Roasted Maple
Sweet Potato & Carrot Sticks

2 to 3 medium sweet potatoes
2 to 3 carrots (If you want just sweet potatoes then skip the carrots
    and add more potatoes)
Extra virgin olive oil, as needed
Salt
Pepper
Thyme or favorite seasoning
2 tablespoons maple syrup

Preheat oven and treat a baking dish or cookie sheet with nonstick spray. Rinse and peel sweet potatoes and carrots. Cut sweet potatoes into short, steak fry–style pieces. Cut carrots into long, thin pieces. Brush both with olive oil and sprinkle with salt, pepper and thyme. Bake until they begin to soften, about 10 minutes. Remove from oven, turn, season again and drizzle with syrup. (Don't use too much syrup, just a bit on each piece for flavor, spread with a brush or back side of a spoon.) Bake an additional 10 to 15 minutes until completely cooked with golden brown edges. Serve hot.

Tricia Benson Breast, Fleming Island

Grilled Vidalia Onions

4 large Vidalia onions
2 tablespoons butter
4 beef bouillon cubes

Prepare grill to medium heat or preheat oven to 350°. Cut top off onions and peel without cutting off root end. Using a spoon, cut a small round section from center of the onions. Place ½ tablespoon butter and a bouillon cube in center of each onion. Wrap individually in heavy duty foil and grill or bake 45 minutes. Place onions in a bowl before opening to capture juice.

Onion Pie

2 medium-large Vidalia onions, thinly sliced
3 tablespoons butter
1 (9-inch) deep-dish pie crust, unbaked
3 eggs, beaten
½ cup half-and-half
½ cup sour cream
2 dashes Tabasco sauce
1 cup shredded Cheddar cheese
Salt and pepper to taste

Preheat oven to 450°. Sauté onions in butter over medium heat until limp and transparent; drain well. Cool and place in pie crust. In a bowl, combine eggs, half-and-half and sour cream mixing well. Stir in Tabasco, cheese, salt and pepper. Pour over onions. Bake 20 minutes; reduce oven to 300° and bake an additional 20 to 25 minutes.

Tomato Pie

4 large tomatoes, sliced
12 slices bacon
½ cup minced sweet onion
1 (9-inch) deep-dish pie crust, baked
1 cup shredded sharp Cheddar cheese
1 cup mayonnaise
4 cloves garlic, crushed
Pinch basil

Preheat oven to 350°. Slice tomatoes and lay on paper towels to drain. Cook bacon crunchy and remove from skillet to drain. Cook onion in bacon grease until soft. Layer tomato slices in pie crust. Chop bacon and sprinkle on top. Sprinkle onion on top. In a small bowl, combine cheese, mayonnaise, garlic and basil; mix well. Spread over top of pie. Bake 35 minutes. Serve warm.

Potato & Tomato Casserole

I'm a vegetarian, and I love this recipe. It was passed down to my husband from his late mom, and I have been making it for us for the last seventeen years. I suggest serving it hot with fresh, cooked asparagus as a side.

1½ pounds potatoes, peeled and
  sliced thin
2 cups chopped tomatoes
1½ cups thinly sliced carrots
½ cup chopped onion

½ clove garlic, minced
¼ cup chopped fresh parsley
Salt and pepper
¼ cup olive oil
Lightly buttered breadcrumbs

Spread potatoes in buttered 9x12-inch baking dish. Mix together tomatoes, carrots, onion, garlic and parsley. Add 1½ cups water. Salt and pepper to taste. Spread mixture evenly over potatoes. Bake at 375° for 1 hour. (Test potatoes with fork to make sure they're soft and done.) Pour oil over top and sprinkle with breadcrumbs. Bake 15 minutes longer until breadcrumbs are golden.

Janice Nearing, Maitland
Save the Manatee Club

Roasted Garlic Tomatoes

12 plum tomatoes, halved lengthwise
4 tablespoons olive oil
1½ tablespoons balsamic vinegar
2 cloves garlic, minced
2 teaspoons sugar
1½ teaspoons kosher salt
½ teaspoon freshly ground black pepper
1 cup chopped fresh basil

Preheat oven to 450°. Arrange tomatoes, cut side up, on a sheet pan. Drizzle with olive oil and balsamic vinegar. Sprinkle with garlic, sugar, salt, pepper and basil. Roast 25 to 30 minutes or until tops are caramelized.

Pecan-Roasted Brussels Sprouts

2 pounds Brussels sprouts, trimmed and halved
4 tablespoons olive oil
2 tablespoons chopped fresh rosemary
Kosher salt, to taste
Freshly ground black pepper, to taste
½ cup chopped pecans
1 pound bacon, cooked crisp and chopped
⅓ cup grated Romano cheese

Preheat oven to 400°. Add Brussels sprouts to a large mixing bowl; add olive oil, rosemary, salt and pepper. Toss well. Line a baking sheet with foil and treat with nonstick spray. Pour Brussels sprout mixture onto tray. Roast 15 minutes, turning twice. Reduce heat to 325°. Add pecans to pan and continue to bake until pecans are roasted and sprouts are lightly brown and crisp. Top with bacon, cheese, salt and pepper to taste. Serve hot.

Spinach & Mushrooms

1 teaspoon butter
1 teaspoon extra virgin olive oil
1 cup sliced baby portobello mushrooms
½ cup thinly sliced leek
1 teaspoon minced garlic
¼ cup vegetable stock
1 tablespoon heavy whipping cream
1 teaspoon fresh lemon juice
⅛ teaspoon salt
2 cups baby spinach
¼ cup grated Parmesan cheese

In a large skillet, melt butter and olive oil together over medium-high heat. Add mushrooms; cook 4 minutes. Add leeks and garlic; cook 3 minutes or until tender. Add stock, cream, lemon juice and salt; cook 2 minutes. Add spinach and cook, stirring frequently, until spinach is wilted, about 2 minutes. Add cheese, stirring until combined. Serves 2.

Vegetarian Moussaka

I loved my grandmother's moussaka. This vegetarian version is just as good.

- 1 medium eggplant, peeled and sliced
- Salt
- 1 pound zucchini, sliced
- ½ cup plus 1 teaspoon vegetable oil
- 2 medium onions, sliced
- 1 (16-ounce) can chopped tomatoes
- ⅛ teaspoon black pepper
- Garlic salt to taste
- ¼ cup milk
- 1 egg
- 1 (8-ounce) package penne pasta, cooked al dente
- 1 tablespoon grated Parmesan cheese
- 2 tablespoons minced fresh parsley
- 1 cup shredded mozzarella cheese

Preheat oven to 350°. Place eggplant slices in a colander and sprinkle with salt. Set aside for 20 minutes. Rinse with cold water to remove all salt. Lightly squeeze slices to remove excess water. Place on large baking sheet treated with nonstick spray. Add zucchini to baking pan ensuring vegetables are in 1 layer. Drizzle with ½ cup oil. Bake until golden brown, 10 minutes on each side. Set aside. In a skillet over medium heat, sauté onion in remaining 1 teaspoon oil about 5 minutes or until golden brown. Drain tomatoes, reserving juice. Add pepper and garlic salt to reserved juice; set aside. In a bowl, beat milk and egg. Add pasta and stir to fully coat. Butter a 9x13-inch pan. Pour pasta into bottom of pan and sprinkle with Parmesan. Layer on eggplant, onion, parsley, zucchini and tomatoes. Pour reserved tomato juice over top and sprinkle with mozzarella. Bake 30 minutes. Rest 10 minutes before cutting. Serves 6.

Florida Wildflower Honey-Glazed Carrots

1 tablespoon butter
1 leek, white part only, halved, thinly
   sliced and washed thoroughly
1 pound Florida carrots, sliced
1 cup Florida orange juice

¼ cup Florida wildflower honey
1 cinnamon stick
2 teaspoons chopped fresh Florida mint
Juice of 2 small lemons
¼ teaspoon kosher salt

Melt butter in a medium saucepan over medium-high heat. Add leek and cook 2 minutes or until lightly browned. Reduce heat to medium. Add carrots and cook 2 minutes or until lightly browned. Add remaining ingredients and bring to a boil. Reduce heat to low, cover and simmer 15 minutes or until carrots are soft. Discard cinnamon stick before serving.

TIP: If you can't find leeks, you can substitute sliced onion.

www.freshfromflorida.com

Turnip & Carrot Mash

2 large turnips, peeled and chopped
6 carrots, peeled and chopped
½ cup butter
½ cup packed light brown sugar
1 teaspoon salt

Place turnips and carrots in a medium-size saucepan and cover with water; bring to a boil over high heat. Reduce heat to medium and cook until tender; drain. Add butter, sugar and salt; mash with a potato masher. Serve hot.

Copper Penny Carrots

A classic recipe that never goes out of style. Delicious!

- 1 pound carrots, cleaned, sliced and cooked
- 1 onion, chopped
- 1 green pepper, chopped
- 1 (10.75-ounce) can tomato soup
- ¼ cup olive oil
- ¼ cup vinegar
- ¾ cup sugar
- 1 teaspoon Worcestershire sauce
- 1 teaspoon prepared mustard
- Dash hot pepper sauce
- Salt and pepper to taste

Place vegetables in a 2-quart baking dish. Mix soup, oil, vinegar, sugar and seasonings. Pour over vegetables and let stand in refrigerator overnight. Delicious served cold or hot.

Asparagus Casserole

1 (16-ounce) can asparagus, drained
2 hard-boiled eggs, sliced
1 (16-ounce) can green peas, drained
¼ cup shredded Cheddar cheese
1 (10.75-ounce) can cream of mushroom soup
½ cup milk
1 cup breadcrumbs
2 tablespoons butter, sliced

Preheat oven to 325°. Place asparagus in a 3-quart baking dish. Layer on eggs, peas and cheese. Combine soup and milk; pour over casserole. Top with breadcrumbs and pats of butter. Bake 25 minutes.

Collards & Cornmeal Dumplings

Collards:

1 ham hock
1 quart chicken stock
1 teaspoon hot sauce
1 teaspoon seasoned salt
1 bunch collard greens
4 tablespoons butter

To a large pot over medium heat, add ham hock, chicken stock, 1 quart water, hot sauce and seasoned salt. Cook 20 minutes. Clean collards very well removing any tough center stems. Roll and cut into strips. Add collards to pot and cook, stirring occasionally, until tender, about 20 minutes. Stir in butter. Using metal tongs, remove and discard ham hock. Remove collards to a serving bowl reserving liquid in pot.

Dumplings:

1½ cups cornmeal
1 cup all-purpose flour
1 small onion, minced
½ teaspoon salt
¼ teaspoon black pepper

Combine dumpling ingredients in a bowl. Stir in ½ cup pot liquor (collard cooking liquid); stir to form a thick batter. Bring pot liquor back to boil over high heat; reduce to medium low. Drop dumpling batter into pot 1 teaspoon at a time. Simmer until cooked through, 20 to 25 minutes. Stir carefully to avoid damaging dumplings. Serve collards topped with juice and dumplings.

Macaroni & Cheese with a Cuban Flavor

4 to 5 slices Cuban bread (can substitute French or Italian bread)
1 pound penne pasta
1 stick Cabot salted butter
1 cup King Arthur unbleached all-purpose flour
4 cups hot milk
1 tablespoon dry mustard
1 tablespoon hot sauce or to taste
1 pound Cabot extra sharp Cheddar cheese, grated (about 4 cups)
¼ pound sliced ham, cut into ½-inch pieces
¼ pound sliced pork, cut into ½-inch pieces
½ cup chopped dill pickles, cut into ½-inch pieces

Preheat oven to 350°. Lightly grease a 9x13-inch baking pan or treat with cooking spray. Place bread slices on a baking sheet and bake 4 to 5 minutes or until lightly browned. Cool, then process in food processor or crush into thick crumbs using a plastic bag (about 1 cup is needed). Cook pasta per package instructions to al dente. Drain well; put it in a large bowl and set aside. Melt butter in saucepan over medium heat; stir in flour until well blended. Continue to cook, stirring constantly, about 2 minutes. (Do not let the mixture turn brown.) Slowly whisk in milk and cook, stirring very frequently, about 4 minutes. Add mustard and hot sauce and stir until incorporated. Add cheese, stir until melted and thoroughly mixed. Lower heat to low and continue to cook, stirring, 3 to 4 more minutes. Add half the sauce to pasta. Add ham, pork and pickles; mix well. Add remaining cheese sauce and mix well. Pour into prepared pan. Spread breadcrumbs evenly over top. Bake 20 to 25 minutes or until hot and bubbly.

Florida Dairy Farmers, Altamonte Springs

Aunt Bunny's Brown Rice Casserole

Aunt Bunny was quite the character. She lived in Jacksonville, where I was born. She was born in Tennessee and her birth name was Daisy Mae. Apparently, she didn't like that, so when she turned 18, she changed her name legally to Bunny Angela. Aunt Bunny was fun—and built. She loved wearing tight T-shirts, which was quite scandalous in the 1960s. She had 10 husbands, one who was a "recycle" as they divorced and remarried later. This is her rice casserole recipe, which is so easy. It was her signature dish.

1 stick butter
1 cup white rice
1 (14.5-ounce) can beef stock
1 (10.5-ounce) can French onion soup
1 (4.5-ounce) jar sliced mushrooms with juice

Preheat oven to 375°. In a bowl, melt butter in microwave. Treat a 9x9-inch baking dish with nonstick spray. Put rice in baking dish; add remaining ingredients including melted butter. (Don't drain the mushrooms. The juice adds more flavor.) Bake about 30 minutes, stir to check doneness, cook additionally until rice has soaked up the liquid – but not dried out. Cover with foil if needed so it does not burn. Serve hot.

Cindy Bruce, Jacksonville

Stick-of-Butter Rice

This is a family favorite at my house. We have it at least once a week. It goes great with any meat—steak, burgers, chicken, or fish.

1 cup rice (uncooked; not instant)
1 (10.5-ounce) can condensed French onion soup
1 (14-ounce) can beef stock
1 stick butter, sliced

Preheat oven to 425°. In a 9x9-inch baking dish combine rice, soup and stock. Place sliced butter on top. Cover with foil and bake 30 minutes. Remove cover and bake another 30 minutes. Serve immediately.

Laurie Paddack Wilkes, Fort Myers

Easy Homestead-Miami Spanish-Style Rice

Homestead Speedway is close to Miami and the Cuban/Spanish influence there is amazing. So, you have to serve up items packed with similar flavors. Now, at home, I would make some serious homemade Spanish-style rice from scratch. But, since this recipe is served up at Homestead or Daytona when I'm serving a slow cooker full of my Chicken Fajita's, I try to stick to easy hot meals with flavor. This recipe is a combo of boxed Spanish rice with my husband's secret to making it taste homemade! Double as needed when you need to feed additional people.

1 (6.8-ounce) box Spanish rice, plus ingredients to prepare per package directions
½ tablespoon powdered chicken bouillon
2 pats real butter

Prepare the Spanish rice as per directions on the package. Then, add in the powdered chicken bouillon and real butter—"not the fake stuff" according to my husband. Before serving, sprinkle additional bouillon in if needed to your taste. It's always a hit.

Jen Jo Cobb, Jennifer Jo Cobb Racing, LLC

Nassau Grits

This dish is excellent with fried fish or shrimp. I make the sauce a day or two ahead and refrigerate. I then make the grits and add sauce before serving.

1 pound bacon
2 green bell peppers, finely chopped
2 medium onions, finely chopped
1½ cups ham, finely chopped
1 (28-ounce) can whole tomatoes, chopped
1 (14-ounce) can whole tomatoes, chopped
1½ cups white quick grits (not instant)

Fry bacon; set aside. Saute bell pepper and onion in 2 to 3 tablespoons bacon drippings until soft. Add ham; saute 15 minutes over low heat. Add tomatoes and simmer 30 minutes. While sauce simmers, cook grits in a separate saucepan according to package directions. When grits are cooked, add sauce and mix well. Serve with bacon crumbled on top. Serves 12.

Brenda Linkous, Pensacola

Beef & Pork

St. Pete Beach Walk

Busy Woman's Roast

1 (3-pound) beef roast
1 (10.75-ounce) can cream of chicken soup
1 (1-ounce) envelope Lipton onion soup mix
2 tablespoons Worcestershire sauce
½ teaspoon each garlic powder, seasoned salt and pepper

Preheat oven to 200°. Place roast on a large aluminum foil sheet. In a small bowl, combine soup, onion soup mix, Worcestershire and seasonings. Spread over roast. Seal foil well so gravy doesn't leak out. Bake 8 to 10 hours. Put Busy Woman's Roast on in the morning and it's ready by dinner time.

Blue Cheese Burger
with Easy Jalapeño Relish

2 pounds ground beef
¼ cup finely chopped onion
3 to 4 tablespoons steak sauce
½ tablespoon minced garlic
2 teaspoons crushed red pepper
Sat and pepper to taste
1 (5-ounce) package blue cheese
1 (8-ounce) jar sweet pickle relish
1 (4-ounce) can chopped jalapeño peppers, drained
1 teaspoon yellow mustard

Combine ground beef in a large bowl with onion, steak sauce, garlic, red pepper, salt and pepper; mix well. Divide into 6 to 8 portions. Cut blue cheese in 6 to 8 squares. Form ground beef into patties around pieces of blue cheese. Grill 8 to 10 minutes or until done. Combine pickle relish, jalapeño peppers and mustard. Spread over hamburger patty and serve on buns with all the fixings.

Garrett Gamble, Key West
Scenic City Yachts

Cheesy Salsa Meatloaf

Growing up, Mom's meatloaf was one of my favorite dishes. It was hearty, filling, and filled the whole house with a fantastic scent that made coming home on a cold day very awesome. This is not her recipe; it's mine. Not as good as mom's but I think I'm getting close.

½ cup milk
2 bread slices (white, wheat or even sourdough)
1½ pounds ground beef
1 cup shredded cheese of your choice
2 eggs, beaten
2 to 3 teaspoons yellow mustard
1 small onion, peeled and fine chopped
½ tablespoon minced garlic
2 teaspoons salt
2 teaspoons black pepper
1 cup salsa, divided

Place milk and bread in a large bowl to soak; break bread into tiny pieces. Add ground beef, cheese, eggs, mustard, onion, seasonings and ½ cup salsa. Using your hands, mix everything together well. Shape into a loaf and place in a greased glass baking dish or on a broiling pan. Bake at 350° for 35 to 45 minutes. Check center for doneness. Before removing from oven, spread remaining salsa over top; sprinkle with additional cheese, if desired. Return to oven and cook another 5 minutes.

Catur Turnbull, Green Cove Springs
United States Navy

Mozzarella-Stuffed Meatloaf

Meatloaf:
1 pound lean ground beef
3 to 4 slices honey wheat bread, toasted and crumbled
1 (1-ounce) envelope onion soup mix
2 medium eggs, beaten
2½ tablespoons Italian seasoning
½ cup milk (or water)
2 tablespoons Worcestershire sauce

Cheese Stuffing:
8 to 10 ounces mozzarella cheese, shredded
¼ cup shredded Cheddar cheese
¼ cup grated Parmesan cheese

Topping Sauce:
1¼ cups ketchup
¼ cup packed brown sugar
1 tablespoon Worcestershire sauce
1 tablespoon red wine vinegar
2 cloves garlic, crushed
Salt and pepper to taste
Red pepper flakes to taste

Preheat oven to 350°; treat a glass baking dish with nonstick spray. Mix Meatloaf ingredients until well combined. Form 2 equal-size flat loaves with a groove down the middle; put bottom loaf in treated baking dish. Combine Cheese Stuffing ingredients and place in groove of bottom loaf. Place remaining loaf over top and pinch edges together to seal. In a bowl, combine Topping Sauce ingredients. Pour half over meatloaf reserving the remaining half. Bake 30 to 40 minutes; remove from oven and top with reserved Topping Sauce. Bake an additional 10 minutes. Serve hot.

Denise Johnson, Melbourne

Mandarin Orange–Ginger Beef Bowls

1½ pounds sirloin steak, sliced thin
5 to 6 green onions, sliced
1 tablespoon ginger powder
½ tablespoon oriental five-spice seasoning
1 red bell pepper, sliced thin
1 green bell pepper, sliced thin
1 small onion, sliced thin
1 (11-ounce) can Mandarin oranges
2 teaspoons cornstarch
1 tablespoon plus ¼ cup soy sauce, divided
2 teaspoons sriracha hot sauce
2 teaspoons sugar
2 teaspoons packed brown sugar
2 tablespoons vegetable oil
1 tablespoon butter
1 (8-ounce) can water chestnuts, drained
½ cup cashew halves
1 (8-ounce) package fried rice, prepared per package directions

Combine steak, scallions, ginger, five-spice seasoning, bell peppers and onion in a large bowl. Drain Mandarin oranges, reserving juice. Add juice to bowl with steak and set oranges aside. In a separate small bowl, combine cornstarch, 1 tablespoon soy sauce, sriracha hot sauce and both sugars. Stir mixture until sugar dissolves. Add to steak and mix well. Cover and chill 30 minutes. Preheat a large skillet with the vegetable oil. Drain beef mixture reserving marinade. Add beef and veggies to skillet and cook, tossing as you go, about 10 minutes. Add reserved marinade and cook until marinade is thickened, and beef is cooked through. Melt butter in a separate small skillet. Add chestnuts, cashews and remaining soy sauce; cook just until heated through. Add reserved Mandarin oranges and mix. Remove from heat. Heat fried rice per package directions. Serve beef over fried rice in a large bowl topped with Mandarin orange mixture.

Wes Locher, Port St. Joe
www.weslocher.com

Cuban-Flavored Grilled Chuck-Eye Steaks

The key to this recipe is letting the steaks marinate overnight. This is especially true when using cheaper and tougher cuts of beef. Serve hot with a side dish like beans or flavored rice.

2 pounds chuck steaks (or your favorite steak)
¼ cup olive oil
1 lime, juiced

1 cup orange juice
1 tablespoon minced garlic
Dried parsley to taste
Salt and pepper to taste

Set steaks out to come to room temperature. Combine remaining ingredients in a large bowl and mix well. Add steaks and turn to coat. Cover and refrigerate overnight. Remove steaks from refrigerator and turn in marinade to be sure they are evenly coated. Grill 15 minutes over hot coals or on a gas grill turning only once. Rest meat 5 minutes before serving.

Tricia Benson Breast, Fleming Island

Seared Steaks with Creamy Ranch Peppercorn Sauce

Creamy Ranch Peppercorn Sauce:

4 tablespoons butter
3 tablespoons flour
1 cup whole milk
1 teaspoon chopped fresh parsley
½ teaspoon chives
¼ teaspoon garlic powder
¼ teaspoon onion powder
½ teaspoon fresh thyme leaves
¼ teaspoon dried rosemary
½ teaspoon salt
1 teaspoon freshly ground black pepper
¼ cup sour cream

Melt butter in a saucepan over medium heat. Stir in flour to make a paste. Stir in milk and cook until mixture thickens, about 5 minutes. Stir in the seasonings and sour cream; mix well.

Seared Steaks:

2 (8-ounce) steaks (1 inch thick)
Salt and pepper to taste
2 tablespoons butter, melted

Season steaks with salt and pepper. Heat a cast-iron skillet over high heat. Brush steaks with 1 tablespoon butter each and cook to preferred temperature. Serve drizzled with Creamy Ranch Peppercorn Sauce.

Florida Dairy Farmers, Altamonte Springs

Bar-B-Que Ribs & More Marinade

This recipe is very simple and uses your favorite barbecue sauce as a base. It's best to marinate ribs at least 3 hours, overnight is better.

½ lemon, juiced
4 tablespoons vinegar
7 tablespoons soy sauce
½ cup barbecue sauce
½ cup ketchup
3 tablespoons packed brown sugar
2 teaspoons salt
2 teaspoons black pepper
2 tablespoons garlic powder

Combine all ingredients in a large bowl or container. Marinate ribs overnight; discard marinade before cooking meat.

Alicia Imperial Lankford, Jacksonville

Chorizo-Stuffed Poblanos

4 poblano peppers
6 ounces (1¼ cups) chorizo sausage
4 ounces (about ¾ cup) Italian or breakfast sausage
4 ounces (1 cup) shredded Cheddar cheese
2 ounces (½ cup) finely chopped mushrooms

Preheat oven to 400°. Remove stems and seeds from peppers. (It's always a good idea to use protective gloves when working with hot peppers.) Place peppers on a baking sheet and roast 20 minutes. Using tongs, give peppers a half turn, then roast another 20 minutes. Skin should be charred and soft. While still hot, place peppers in a zip-close plastic bag for about 10 minutes. Reduce oven to 375°. While peppers rest, brown chorizo and Italian sausage in a skillet over medium heat, breaking meats up as they cook. Drain; add cheese and mushrooms and stir to combine. Remove peppers from bag and remove skin (should be able to simply rub with gloved hands). Place peppers on baking sheet and fill with sausage stuffing. Bake 20 minutes or until internal temperature is 155°. I like to serve these with avocado and tomato salsa and tortilla chips.

Chef Eileen Morris, Crystal Beach
www.personalcheftampabay.com

St. Augustine Lions Seafood Festival

St. Augustine

1st Weekend in March

The St. Augustine Lions Seafood Festival features delicious seafood, more than 100 artists and craftsmen, and an entertainment lineup featuring jazz, country, and Americana music. In downtown St. Augustine, the festival will serve up boatloads of seafood, along with a three-day lineup of entertainment, family fun, and affordable arts and crafts. Eat, drink, and shop till you drop. Family fun can be had in the kidz zone, pirate village, and Spanish landing. Be sure to catch the clown adventure, Mayhem the Pirate Magician, and Nutter Interactive percussion. Kids can also meet their favorite superhero or fairytale princess.

Francis Field • 25 West Castillo Drive • St. Augustine, FL 32084
904.377.4312 • www.lionsfestival.com
Facebook: staugustinelionsfestival

Loin Lamb Chops

¼ cup olive oil
3 tablespoons Dijon mustard
2 cloves garlic, minced
¼ teaspoon dried thyme
2 tablespoons chopped fresh mint leaves
6 lamb chops, trimmed of fat
1 cup panko breadcrumbs
¼ cup melted butter

In a covered container large enough to hold chops, combine oil, mustard, garlic, thyme and mint; mix well. Add chops; cover tightly. Marinate at least 4 hours, flipping every hour. When ready to cook, combine breadcrumbs and butter in a shallow dish. Press chops in crumb mixture. Grill on grill pan sprayed with cooking spray to desired temperature. Grill over medium heat 4 to 5 minutes per side to desired temperature.

Sally Kees, Fernandina Beach

Apple Cider Pork Chops

2 tablespoons olive oil (or butter)
2 cloves garlic, mashed
4 pork loin chops
½ cup apple cider
3 tablespoons butter
4 tablespoons packed brown sugar
1 pound apples, cut into ¾-inch slices
⅓ cup coconut milk
½ tablespoon chopped sage
Salt and pepper

Heat oil in a large skillet over medium heat; add garlic and sauté 1 minute. Add meat, and cook 4 minutes on each side. Add cider and cook until liquid is reduced by half, about 5 minutes. While pork chops cook, melt butter in a saucepan over medium heat. Stir in sugar and cook 1 minute. Add apples and sauté until brown and tender; set aside. Add coconut milk to pork chops and cook another 5 minutes. Add sage and season with salt and pepper to taste. Add cooked apples and mix; serve hot.

Jamie Martin, Newberry
Pampered Chef

Coca-Cola Pork Chops

1 cup ketchup
1 (12-ounce) can Coca-Cola
2 to 4 pork chops

Mix ketchup and Coca-Cola. Place pork chops in a frying pan; pour ketchup mixture over top. Cook on medium heat until pork chops are done. Remove pork chops from heat; plate.   Heat leftover sauce until thickened; pour over pork chops and serve.

Baked Apple Pork Chops & Maple Sauerkraut

Don't worry; this recipe may seem difficult, but it's not. It makes for a wonderful dish that is great during cooler months or all year long when you want something filling.

4 pork loin chops, 1 inch thick
1 (8-ounce) bottle apple juice, divided
Salt and pepper
½ cup apple butter
1 tablespoon Dijon mustard
1 cup breadcrumbs
2 tablespoons olive oil
½ tablespoon minced garlic
½ cup finely chopped sweet onion
½ cup peeled and diced apples
½ cup chopped walnuts or pecans
1 (32-ounce) jar sauerkraut
2½ tablespoons maple syrup

Place pork chops in sealable container. Measure ¼ cup apple juice to use tomorrow. Pour remaining apple juice over pork chops, cover and refrigerate overnight. When ready to cook, remove chops and sprinkle both sides with salt and pepper. Combine apple butter and mustard; spread evenly over chops—top, bottom, sides. Dredge in breadcrumbs to coat. Preheat oven to 350°. Heat oil in a deep skillet; quickly brown chops on both sides (do not fully cook). Remove skillet from heat. Remove chops to a baking dish and bake 15 minutes. While chops are cooking, return skillet to heat; add more oil if needed. Add garlic, onion and apples; sauté lightly to brown apple edges. Add 2 tablespoons (half) reserved apple juice and nuts. Cook until nuts are heated through; remove to a bowl. Add remaining 2 tablespoons apple juice to skillet over medium heat. Stir in sauerkraut and cook until heated through. Stir in maple syrup and remove from heat. To serve, spread apple-nut mixture over each pork chop and serve hot over a bed of sauerkraut.

Denise Johnson, Melbourne

Parmesan-Honey Pork Roast

This is the best tasting pork I have ever eaten. As a working mom, I love that it is super easy to make.

1¾ pounds boneless pork loin roast
⅔ cup grated Parmesan cheese
½ cup honey
3 tablespoons soy sauce
1 tablespoon dried basil
1 tablespoon dried oregano
2 tablespoons chopped garlic
2 tablespoons olive oil
½ teaspoon salt
2 tablespoons cornstarch
¼ cup chicken stock

Place roast in slow cooker. In a bowl, combine cheese, honey, soy sauce, basil, oregano, garlic, oil and salt. Pour over roast. Cover and cook on low 5 to 6 hours. Remove meat and place on platter. Strain juices into a saucepan over medium heat. Mix cornstarch and chicken stock together. Add to saucepan and cook until thickened. Serve over sliced roast.

Laurie Paddack Wilkes, Fort Myers

Polynesian Pork Loin

½ teaspoon salt
½ teaspoon pepper
1 (4-pound) boneless pork loin
1 (8-ounce) can crushed pineapple with juice
1 cup Russian salad dressing
1 (1-ounce) envelope onion soup mix
¼ cup packed brown sugar
¼ cup apricot preserves

Preheat oven to 350°. Rub salt and pepper over pork loin; place in a shallow roasting pan. Bake uncovered 1 hour. In a saucepan, combine 1 cup water, pineapple, salad dressing, onion soup mix, brown sugar and apricot preserves; heat until well mixed. Pour over roast. Bake another 1½ to 2 hours, or until meat thermometer reads 160°, basting occasionally. Let stand 15 minutes before slicing. Use sauce to serve over meat.

Steinhatchee Fiddler Crab Festival, Steinhatchee

Steinhatchee Fiddler Crab Festival

Steinhatchee • Presidents' Day Weekend

First held in 2008, the Steinhatchee Fiddler Crab Festival boasts delicious food and unmatched fun. Enjoy delicious seafood while you shop the various arts and crafts vendors. Visitors will also enjoy live entertainment from well-known bands and solo artists, and if you're feeling bold, you can even take the stage yourself during the open mic talent show. Watch the parade, tour a car show, take a river tour, and sample cook-off dishes. It's all about da crab!

Downtown Steinhatchee • Steinhatchee, FL 32359
352.356.8185 • www.steinhatcheechamber.com
Facebook: SteinhatcheeChamber

Pork Loin Roast Stuffed with Chutney & Apple

1 pork loin
1 (4-ounce) jar Jacquie's Jamming Chutney
1 Granny Smith apple, peeled and thinly sliced
Salt and fresh ground pepper
Olive oil

Preheat oven to 450°. Measure 5 to 7 pieces of butcher's twine long enough to tie around pork loin. Spread twine across roasting pan, evenly spaced. Butterfly loin and place, open, over twine in pan. Spread chutney liberally over both open sides of loin. Add sliced apple to 1 side and lightly salt and pepper to taste. Close loin and tie twine tight to seal. Add more salt and pepper to outside. Drizzle with olive oil and rub completely around roll. Bake 20 minutes per pound. When cooked, remove and rest 10 to 15 minutes before slicing.

Jacquie Hoare-Ward, Naples
Jacquie's Jamming Jams

Bean Chalupa

My family loves this dish. My mother always made it for our birthday parties and other special family gatherings. It's hearty and serves a crowd. It's similar to a taco salad.

1 pound dried pinto beans
1 (3-pound) pork roast
1 onion, chopped
2 cloves garlic
1 tablespoon salt
2 tablespoons chili powder
1 tablespoon ground cumin
1 teaspoon dried oregano
2 (4-ounce) cans chopped green chile peppers, drained
½ (8-ounce) jar medium-heat taco sauce
Black olives, lettuce, cheese, avocado, tomatoes and jalapeños for topping

Place all ingredients, except taco sauce, in a slow cooker. Stir in 7 cups water. Cook on high 5 hours. Shred roast and add taco sauce. Serve over corn chips and add toppings if desired.

John Breast, Jacksonville

Quick Grilling Sauce

This is great with everything from steak and burgers to chicken, pork and even grilled tuna and shark steaks.

1 large onion, chopped
¼ cup vegetable oil
1 (8-ounce) can tomato sauce
¼ cup lemon juice
¼ cup firmly packed brown sugar
3 tablespoons Worcestershire sauce
2 tablespoons Dijon mustard
2 teaspoons salt
¼ teaspoon pepper

Combine all ingredients in a saucepan over medium heat. Add ½ cup water and mix well. Simmer 30 minutes before using as a baste or sauce for hamburgers, steaks and more.

Garrett Gamble, Key West
Scenic City Yachts

Sweet Pickle Relish Hot Dog Topping

When Stephanie Owler Loudermilk of Titusville shared some recipes, her daughter Jade also wanted a recipe of her own to be included in the *Florida Hometown Cookbook*. Here is Jade's recipe for her favorite hot dog topping. Try it with hamburgers and even crab cakes.

3 tablespoons ketchup
3 tablespoons sweet relish
3 tablespoons mustard
2 tablespoons mayonnaise
½ cup chopped tomato
¼ cup chopped red onion

Mix in a bowl and serve with hot dogs.

Jade, Titusville

Chicken & Other Poultry

Jacksonville Skyline

Arroz con Pollo

1 to 2 tablespoons butter
2 pounds boneless chicken pieces
½ tablespoon minced garlic
1 medium onion, chopped
1 large green bell pepper, chopped
1 (14.5-ounce) can chicken stock
1 (6.8-ounce) box Rice-A-Roni Rice & Vermicelli Mix
1 tomato, coarsely chopped
1 to 2 teaspoons red pepper flakes

Melt butter in a large covered skillet; add chicken pieces and garlic. Cook until chicken is browned; chop and return to skillet. Stir in onion and bell pepper. Continue cooking about 5 minutes while stirring. Add ½ cup water and chicken stock. Bring to a boil; reduce heat to low. Add rice mix and seasoning packet. Stir, cover and cook about 15 minutes or until rice is soft. Stir in chopped tomatoes and red pepper flakes. Serve hot.

Heather Kirby, Fort Lauderdale

The Original Marathon Seafood Festival

Marathon • 2nd Weekend in March

The Original Marathon Seafood Festival is truly a family-friendly event. The event features fresh-caught local Keys seafood at amazing prices, cold beverages for adults and kids, live entertainment the entire weekend, more than 220 vendors, a boat and art show, and plenty of rides and games for children.

Marathon Community Park • Marathon, FL 33050
305.743.5417 • www.MarathonSeafoodFestival.com
Facebook: The Original Marathon Seafood Festival

Baked Chicken Tender Po'boys with Honey-Dijon Sauce

10 to 12 chicken strips
½ cup French dressing
1 (4.5-ounce) box Kraft Shake 'n Bake Original Chicken Seasoned Coating Mix
4 hoagie buns
Butter for toasting
½ cup Dijon mustard
2 tablespoons honey
Sliced onions, tomato and lettuce for topping

Preheat oven 425°. Coat tenders with French dressing. Roll in chicken coating mixture and place on a treated baking sheet. Bake 15 to 20 minutes, or until chicken is done. Spread hoagie buns with butter and toast. Mix mustard and honey in a bowl and spread over buns. Add cooked chicken and top with onions, tomato and lettuce. Serve immediately.

Damon Barfield, Green Cove Springs

Apricot Salsa Chicken

½ cup flour
¼ teaspoon pepper
1 teaspoon salt
¼ teaspoon paprika
6 boneless, skinless chicken breasts
3 tablespoons vegetable oil
1 (16-ounce) jar salsa
1 (12-ounce) jar apricot preserves
½ cup apricot nectar (or juice from canned apricots)

In a shallow bowl, combine flour and seasonings. Dredge chicken in flour until well coated. Brown chicken in hot oil. Remove chicken and pour remaining oil from pan. Add chicken back to pan along with salsa, preserves, and nectar; bring to a boil. Reduce heat; simmer, uncovered, 15 minutes or until sauce thickens and meat juices run clear. Serve hot over cooked rice. Serves 4 to 6.

Cuban-Style Shredded Chicken with Black Beans & Rice

This recipe will seem long due to the ingredients, but it's not. Just think of it this way—chicken with a bunch of seasoning, then some beans, and then some rice!

Chicken:

3 tablespoons vegetable oil plus more for cooking
2 tablespoons ground cumin
1 tablespoon chili powder
1 tablespoon Italian seasoning
2 teaspoons seasoned salt
2 to 3 teaspoons minced garlic
¼ cup orange juice
2 teaspoons lime juice
2 chicken breasts

Combine all the ingredients except chicken in a food processor or blender; process to create a marinade. Add chicken to a lidded dish, add marinade, cover and refrigerate overnight. Heat a large skillet with vegetable oil over medium-high heat. Once hot, add chicken and cook 10 to 12 minutes or until browned all over and cooked through. Add remaining marinade to skillet and cook 5 minutes or until slightly reduced.

Beans:

2 teaspoons vegetable oil
½ yellow onion, diced
3 cloves garlic, minced
2 (15.25-ounce) cans black beans, drained
2 teaspoons ground cumin powder
2 teaspoons paprika
2 teaspoons garlic powder
Salt and pepper to taste

Heat vegetable oil in a large cast-iron skillet over medium-high heat. Add onion and sauté 3 to 4 minutes or until soft and translucent. Add garlic and sauté 30 to 60 seconds. Add black beans and seasonings and cook 5 to 10 minutes. Using a potato masher, mash about half of the beans in the pan, then stir well. Season with salt and pepper if necessary.

Cilantro-Lime Rice:

1 teaspoon vegetable oil
½ yellow onion, diced
1½ cups jasmine rice
3 cups low-sodium chicken stock
2 limes, juiced
½ cup fresh cilantro, chopped
Salt and pepper to taste

Heat vegetable oil in a large saucepan over medium-high heat. Add onion and sauté until soft. Add rice and stir to coat with the oil; cook about 1 minute. Add chicken stock; bring to a boil. Reduce heat to a simmer and place lid on pan. Cook about 15 minutes or until most of the liquid has absorbed. Turn off heat and allow rice to sit, covered, an additional 5 minutes. Add lime juice, cilantro, salt and pepper. To serve, divide Cilantro-Lime Rice among bowls. Top with chicken and black beans.

Millie Johnson, Melbourne

Downtown Melbourne

Chicken Pot Pie

3 chicken breasts, chopped
2 cups sliced carrots
2 cups diced potatoes
2 cups diced onions
1 (8-ounce) can Le Sueur peas, drained
1 (10.75-ounce) can cream of
  chicken soup
1 (10.75-ounce) can cream of
  celery soup
½ cup chicken stock
1 stick margarine, melted
1 cup self-rising flour
1 cup milk

Preheat oven to 350°. Cook chicken breasts, carrots, potatoes and onions in salted water to cover 15 to 20 minutes, until chicken is cooked and vegetables are tender. Drain well. Line the bottom of a 9x13-inch dish with chicken. Layer cooked vegetables on top. Top with peas. In a separate bowl, combine soups and chicken stock. Pour over chicken. Mix margarine, flour and milk. Pour over casserole. Bake 30 minutes; increase temperature to 375° and bake 15 minutes.

Banana Salsa Chicken

Banana Salsa:

3 bananas, sliced
⅓ cup chopped red bell pepper
⅓ cup chopped yellow bell pepper
1 jalapeño pepper, seeded and chopped
3 tablespoons chopped cilantro
1½ limes, juiced
1½ tablespoons packed brown sugar
Salt and pepper to taste

Combine Banana Salsa ingredients in a bowl; mix well. Let rest 1 hour or longer.

Chicken:

1 egg
½ cup milk
1½ cups breadcrumbs
1½ cups chopped toasted pecans
6 boneless, skinless chicken breasts
Salt and pepper to taste
3 tablespoons Dijon mustard
½ cup flour
3 tablespoons vegetable oil

Preheat oven to 350°. In a medium bowl, beat egg with milk. In a separate medium bowl, mix breadcrumbs and pecans. Season chicken with salt and pepper. Spread with Dijon mustard and coat lightly with flour. Dip into egg mixture, then pecan mixture, pressing to coat well. Heat oil in a nonstick sauté pan. Sauté chicken until golden brown on both sides, turning once. Remove to a baking dish. Bake 15 to 20 minutes or until cooked through. Serve topped with Banana Salsa. Serves 6.

Feta- & Tomato-Stuffed Chicken Breasts

1 (8-ounce) jar sun-dried tomatoes packed in oil
½ cup finely chopped red onion
2 tablespoons olive oil, divided
1½ teaspoons minced garlic
¼ cup pine nuts, lightly toasted
¼ pound feta cheese, crumbled (approximately 1 cup)
2 tablespoons grated Parmesan cheese
1 tablespoon fresh marjoram (or 1 teaspoon dried)
Salt and pepper to taste
2 whole boneless chicken breasts, halved

Drain tomatoes in a colander; rinse and set aside to dry. Sauté onion in 1 tablespoon oil in a medium saucepan over moderate heat, stirring until softened. Add garlic and cook an additional minute. Stir in pine nuts, tomatoes, cheeses and marjoram; season with salt and pepper. Preheat oven to 350°. Insert knife into thicker end of each chicken breast and cut a lengthwise pocket, making it as wide as possible. Fill each breast with ¼ cup filling. Heat remaining 1 tablespoon oil in large skillet until hot; brown chicken 5 minutes each side. Place in baking dish and bake 20 minutes or until just cooked through. Serves 4.

GastroFest

Jacksonville • Mid March

GastroFest celebrates the food culture of the First Coast with tastes from local restaurants, food trucks, and caterers. The GastroFest Marketplace features food artisans from around the First Coast, selling everything from baked goods and preserves to honey, tea, and spices. The festival also includes free educational components with panels and talks throughout the day, local beers, spirits, and more.

Hemming Park
135 West Monroe Street
Jacksonville, FL 32202
352.207.4450 • www.gastrojax.org
Facebook: Gastrojax

Fiesta Chicken

2 chickens, cut up
1 small head garlic, minced
2 tablespoons fresh oregano
1 teaspoon salt
½ teaspoon freshly ground pepper
¼ cup red wine vinegar
¼ cup olive oil

¼ cup pitted green Spanish olives
1 cup sliced fresh mushrooms
¼ cup capers with 1 tablespoon juice
2 to 3 bay leaves
½ cup packed light brown sugar
½ cup white wine
2 tablespoons minced fresh parsley

In a large bowl, combine chicken pieces, garlic, oregano, salt, pepper, wine vinegar, olive oil, olives, mushrooms, capers with juice and bay leaves. Cover and marinate in refrigerator overnight. Preheat oven to 350°. Arrange chicken in a single layer on a large baking pan; spoon marinade over each piece then sprinkle with brown sugar. Pour wine around chicken. Bake 50 minutes, basting frequently with pan juices. Transfer chicken, olives, mushrooms and capers to a serving dish. Spoon pan juices over chicken and sprinkle with parsley. Serves 6.

Island Chicken

1 (25-ounce) bottle white wine
3 boneless, skinless chicken breasts, quartered
4 ounces butter
4 cloves garlic, crushed
1 cup orange juice
2 tablespoons soy sauce
¼ teaspoon ground cinnamon
2 medium mangoes, peeled and sliced lengthwise into spears

Pour wine into a large skillet over high heat. Add chicken and poach about 7 minutes. Pour off liquid reserving 1 cup. Reduce heat to medium. Add butter and garlic to pan and slowly pan-fry chicken until brown, about 5 minutes per side. Return reserved liquid to pan along with orange juice, soy sauce, cinnamon and mangoes. Cover and simmer 10 minutes or until chicken is completely cooked. Makes 4 servings.

Captain Todd's Teriyaki Duck or Chicken Tacos

Captain Jordan Todd is a third-generation fisherman, born and raised along the Gulf Coast of Florida. He says his passion for the area led him to earn his degree in marine biology and more. "I love all things fishing and wildlife," Todd says. "That's why I started Saltwater Obsessions. I wanted to start a guide service where I could provide my customers a fun time packed with memories. It's a passion—it really is. They're not just customers. They become friends. I hope they leave knowing that I had a great time being with them, catching fish off the coast of Port St. Joe or along the bays and canals." Jordan is an avid sportsman and figured everyone would send in fish and seafood recipes, so he shared this easy taco that's perfect with duck or chicken breasts.

4 to 5 duck breasts (or an equal portion of chicken breasts)
½ cup teriyaki sauce
½ cup sesame garlic sauce
8 pieces bacon
½ large onion, chopped
Tortilla shells
Shredded Cheddar cheese, chopped avocado, salsa, chopped peppers and sour cream for toppings

Cut duck into strips and place in zip-close bag. Add teriyaki and sesame garlic sauce; marinate 8 to 10 hours (or 4 to 5 hours if using chicken). When ready to cook, add bacon to a large skillet over medium-high heat and cook until crisp; remove from skillet. Sauté onion in bacon grease until caramelized; add in the duck strips and stir until cooked through. When done, serve on tortilla shells with onion, bacon and other toppings of choice. I like using cheese, avocado, salsa, peppers and sour cream.

Captain Jordan Todd, Port St. Joe
Saltwater Obsessions Guide Service

Coconut Chicken with Tropical Aioli Sauce

8 chicken tenders
1½ cups panko breadcrumbs
½ teaspoon garlic powder
¼ teaspoon onion powder
Salt and pepper to taste
⅓ cup shredded coconut
3 eggs
¼ cup coconut milk
Oil for frying

Cut chicken in half lengthwise. Combine breadcrumbs, garlic powder, onion power, salt, pepper and coconut in a bowl; set aside. In a separate bowl, beat eggs; stir in coconut milk. Dip chicken strips in egg mixture, then dredge in breadcrumbs to evenly coat. Place (without touching) on a cookie sheet lined with parchment paper and freeze 30 minutes. While chicken is in freezer, make Tropical Aioli Sauce. When ready to serve, fry chicken in 1½ inches oil at 350° for 2 minutes per side until golden brown and cooked through. Drain on paper towels. Serve hot with Tropical Aioli Sauce on the side.

Tropical Aioli Sauce:

1 (8-ounce) can crushed pineapple, drained
2 tablespoons mango jam
1 teaspoon yellow mustard
1 cup mayonnaise
½ cup sour cream

Mix all ingredients and chill until ready to serve.

Phyllis Sullivan, Palm Bay

Balsamic Chicken

1 teaspoon garlic powder
1 teaspoon dried basil
½ teaspoon salt
½ teaspoon pepper
2 teaspoons dried minced onion
1 tablespoon extra virgin olive oil
4 cloves garlic, minced
8 boneless, skinless chicken thighs
½ cup balsamic vinegar

Combine first 5 ingredients in a small bowl; set aside. Add olive oil and garlic to slow cooker. Cover chicken with spice mixture and place in slow cooker. Pour balsamic vinegar over chicken. Cover and cook on high 4 hours. Serve with rice or potatoes.

Laurie Paddack Wilkes, Fort Myers

Tallahassee Chain of Parks

Honey-Garlic Chicken

4 boneless, skinless chicken thighs
2 cloves garlic, minced
⅓ cup honey
½ cup ketchup
½ cup soy sauce
½ teaspoon dried oregano
2 tablespoons minced parsley
½ tablespoon toasted sesame seeds, optional

Place chicken thighs in slow cooker. In a small bowl, combine garlic, honey, ketchup, soy sauce, oregano and parsley. Pour over chicken. Cover and cook on low 4 to 5 hours (or high 3 to 4 hours). Remove chicken to a serving platter; spoon sauce over chicken and sprinkle with sesame seeds.

Laurie Paddack Wilkes, Fort Myers

Slow-Cooker Chicken with Catalina-Apricot Glaze

6 frozen boneless, skinless chicken breasts (not thawed)
Salt and pepper
1 red bell pepper, cubed 1-inch pieces
1 yellow bell pepper, cubed 1-inch pieces
1 small onion, large chopped
1 (10-ounce) jar apricot preserves
1 (16-ounce) bottle Catalina dressing
1 (1-ounce) envelope onion soup mix
2 tablespoons minced garlic
2 tablespoons Heinz 57 sauce
½ cup Coca-Cola

Spray slow cooker with nonstick spray or use a slow cooker bag. Place chicken into slow cooker and season to taste with salt and pepper. Add peppers and onion. In a separate bowl, combine preserves, dressing, soup mix, garlic, 57 sauce and Coca-Cola. Mix well and pour over chicken. Cook on low 6 to 7 hours. Delicious served over brown or wild rice.

Tricia Benson Breast, Fleming Island

Honeyed Teriyaki Chicken

2 pounds boneless, skinless chicken
   breasts
Oil for frying
2 large eggs, beaten

½ cup all-purpose flour
½ teaspoon salt
⅛ teaspoon black pepper
2 tablespoons sesame seeds

Cut chicken into 1-inch cubes. Heat oil in a shallow skillet over medium heat. Place eggs in a shallow bowl. Combine flour, salt and pepper in another shallow bowl. Dip chicken in egg; coat with flour mixture. When oil is hot, cook chicken, in small batches, until brown. Prepare Honeyed Teriyaki Glaze. Place cooked chicken in glaze, stirring to coat completely. Spoon chicken into a baking pan, reserving remaining glaze in saucepan. Place in oven and sprinkle top with sesame seeds. Bake at 250° for 10 minutes; remove chicken from oven. Brush with reserved sauce; cook another 10 minutes. Serves 4.

Honeyed Teriyaki Glaze:

    ⅓ cup soy sauce
    ⅓ cup honey
    1 tablespoon sherry (or 1 tablespoon sugar)
    1 clove garlic, crushed
    1 teaspoon freshly grated ginger

Combine ingredients in a small saucepan over medium heat. Stir well and cook until heated through and fully combined.

Adobo Pork & Chicken

This recipe is for a rich adobo sauce that is wonderful for chicken or pork (separately or combined). You can use a variety of cuts; I prefer leg quarters when using chicken and country-style pork ribs when using pork.

½ pound cubed pork
½ pound cubed chicken
Oil for browning
½ onion, sliced
3 to 4 cloves garlic, minced
4 tablespoons vinegar
4 tablespoons soy sauce
2 tablespoons Pufina Patis fish sauce
½ teaspoon packed brown sugar
4 small potatoes, quartered
½ cup frozen green peas
3 carrots, cut 1-inch thick
3 celery sticks, cut 1-inch thick

Use a deep-sided skillet large enough to hold everything. Quickly brown pork and chicken in hot oil; remove to drain. To same skillet, add onion and garlic; sauté 2 minutes. Add vinegar, soy sauce, fish sauce and brown sugar. Add browned pork and cook 35 minutes, adding water as needed. Add chicken and cook an additional 20 minutes, adding water as needed. Add vegetables and cook another 20 minutes or until potatoes and carrots are tender. Serve hot with white rice.

Alicia Imperial Lankford, Jacksonville

Jen's Daytona Racing Chicken Fajitas

Jen Jo Cobb is more than a NASCAR driver. She's also the owner of a two-truck team in the NASCAR Camping World Truck Series and car owner in the ARCA Racing Series. And, she's often the team chef, saying, "I cook a lot of meals for our team and this is one of my favorites for a large group like we would have at a race like Daytona."

1 pound boneless, skinless chicken breasts
1 (1-ounce) envelope fajita seasoning
1 to 2 (10-ounce) cans Rotel tomatoes
1 (8-ounce) package shredded Cheddar cheese
12 to 24 small tortillas

Put chicken and fajita seasoning in a slow cooker (use slow cooker liners; amazing invention); cook on low 4 hours. Add tomatoes and cook another 2 to 4 hours or until chicken shreds easily with a fork. Remove to serving bowl and top with cheese. Serve hot with warmed tortillas.

Jen Jo Cobb, Jennifer Jo Cobb Racing, LLC

South Florida Garlic Fest

Lake Worth • 2nd Weekend in February

Affectionately named "The Best Stinkin' Party" in Florida, the South Florida Garlic Fest showcases the epitome of homegrown talent and cultural celebration, providing an outlet for local artists and chefs to express themselves. The event is dedicated to exploring the numerous health and culinary possibilities of garlic. Countless recipes and unique dishes have been created by professional chefs in the Garlic Chef cooking competition and by our Gourmet Alley concessionaires, including garlic ice cream, Argentinean garlic BBQ, and Garlic Fest crab cakes. Come out for tasty food and live entertainment while supporting art and education for local youth.

John Prince Park • 2700 6th Avenue South • Lake Worth, FL 33461
561.279.0907 • www.garlicfestfl.com
Facebook: GarlicFestFL

Mike Surman's Favorite Chicken Casserole

When I'm traveling around the country on the FLW Tour, I need something that can be quickly reheated and is delicious after a long day on the water. This recipe definitely fits the bill. Enjoy.

2 to 4 chicken breasts, cooked and cubed
1 (16-ounce) container sour cream
1 (10.75-ounce) can cream of mushroom soup
1 (4-ounce) can chopped mushrooms, drained
2 to 3 tablespoons margarine
1 (14-ounce) package herb stuffing, divided

Combine chicken breasts, sour cream, soup and mushrooms in a baking dish. Melt margarine with 2 tablespoons water. Stir in three quarters of the dry stuffing mix. Stir into chicken mixture. Sprinkle remaining dry stuffing over top; cover with foil. Bake at 350° for 50 minutes. Remove foil and bake another 5 to 10 minutes or until topping is crisp.

Mike Surman, professional bass angler, Boca Raton

Orange Chicken

We're open daily for tours, and while visitors are taste testing, they always ask about food pairings and recipe ideas for our unique wines. This Orange Chicken recipe is delicious, made with our Florida Sunshine Orange Wine.

2 boneless, skinless chicken breasts
Flour to dredge
1 teaspoon olive oil
1 teaspoon minced garlic
1 orange, sliced
1 teaspoon butter
¼ cup Florida Sunshine orange wine
Parsley for garnish

Pound chicken breasts flat; dredge in flour. Heat oil in a sauté pan over medium heat; add garlic and sauté. When garlic starts to brown, add chicken breasts and cover with sliced oranges. Cook 3 to 4 minutes; turn. After 2 minutes, add butter and wine. Spoon sauce over chicken to baste as it cooks. Cook another 4 to 5 minutes or until done. Remove chicken to a serving dish. Discard oranges. Pour sauce from pan over chicken. Garnish with chopped parsley.

Vince Shook, St. Petersburg
Florida Orange Groves Winery

Tropical Wings

5 cups packed brown sugar
5 cups low-sodium soy sauce
1 (20-ounce) can crushed pineapple with juice
¼ cup grated fresh ginger root
1 tablespoon crushed garlic
½ cup deep red wine
1 cup rice vinegar
60 chicken wings

In a large stockpot over low heat, dissolve sugar in soy sauce; mix in pineapple, ginger, garlic, red wine and vinegar. Add wings; simmer 2 hours over low heat. Cool; skim off fat. Grill wings 10 minutes, basting with leftover sauce.

Sue Dannahower, Fort Pierce

Caribbean Chicken

4 chicken breasts
Poultry seasoning or seasoned salt
⅓ cup fresh orange juice
1½ tablespoons olive oil
2 tablespoons lime juice
2 to 3 teaspoons ginger powder
2 to 3 teaspoons chili powder
2 teaspoons hot sauce
2 teaspoons Italian seasoning
¼ cup finely chopped onion
¼ cup finely chopped red bell pepper
½ tablespoon minced jalapeño pepper,
  optional

Rinse chicken and sprinkle with poultry seasoning or seasoned salt to taste. Set aside in a zip-close bag or covered dish. In a blender, combine orange juice, olive oil, lime juice, ginger, chili powder, hot sauce and Italian seasoning. Blend well. Add onion, bell pepper and jalapeño; quickly pulse just enough to mix but not pulverize. Pour over chicken and refrigerate 24 hours; occasionally turn chicken while it marinades. Grill chicken over hot coals about 15 minutes or until completely cooked. Serve hot over rice and beans, grilled mixed vegetables or even mixed salad greens.

Wes Locher, Port St. Joe
www.weslocher.com

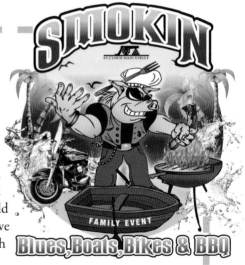

Smokin' Blues, Boats, Bikes & BBQ

Saint Cloud • May

Smokin' Blues, Boats, Bikes & BBQ is a family-friendly annual event located on our beautiful lakefront for all to enjoy. Cardboard boat races, law enforcement motorcycle competition, and people's choice award for best pulled pork add to the flavor of the event. You'll also enjoy live entertainment throughout the day, topped off with the blues headliner in the evening.

1104 Lakeshore Boulevard • Saint Cloud, FL 34769
407.498.0008 • www.stcloudmainstreet.org
Facebook: Saint Cloud Main Street

Grilled Buffalo Chicken Texas Cheese Toast Sandwiches

The secret to this recipe is simple. Combine spicy seasoned chicken, Texas toast and cheese. This is perfect with seasoned rotisserie chicken from your grocery store.

3½ cups shredded rotisserie chicken
½ cup buffalo wing sauce
1 (8-ounce) package cream cheese
½ cup finely chopped onion

½ cup finely chopped green bell pepper
Butter as needed
8 slices Texas toast
8 slices Cheddar cheese

Combine chicken, wing sauce and cream cheese in a bowl. Sauté onion and peppers in butter and stir into chicken mixture. Butter slices toast and break cheese slices into 16 pieces. Make your sandwiches with toast, ½ slice of cheese, chicken mixture, ½ slice of cheese, and top with second piece of toast. Grill in a skillet over medium heat, turning once, until both sides are golden and cheese is melted. Serve hot.

Alan McCall, Tallahassee
WDXD/Big D Country

Ham & Chicken Wraps

¼ pound sliced deli ham, shredded
¼ pound sliced deli chicken, shredded
1 (15-ounce) can black beans, drained
¼ cup chopped onion
1 (8.75-ounce) can whole-kernel corn, drained
1 cup medium-heat salsa
1 (5.6-ounce) package Spanish rice, prepared per package directions
Lime or lemon juice
1 cup shredded Cheddar cheese
10 flour tortillas

Combine ham, chicken, beans, onion, corn and a salsa in a saucepan over medium heat; simmer just until heated through, about 8 minutes. Drizzle prepared Spanish rice with lemon or lime juice and stir. Spoon equal portions of both mixtures onto tortillas; add shredded cheese. Fold to close and serve hot.

Christine Morgan, Pensacola and Panama City

Benjamin's Stuffed Turkey Burgers

My grandson Benjamin, who's fourteen years old, came up with these stuffed cheese burgers. He really enjoys cooking. This recipe uses ground turkey or ground chicken but can also be used with ground beef. The recipe served four people on a recent evening, when Benjamin made them for us. They're big, so one burger apiece was plenty for us.

—Alan McCall

1 pound ground turkey (or chicken or beef)
1 tablespoon salt
1 tablespoon pepper
1½ teaspoons garlic
Liquid smoke to taste
Four slices of your favorite cheese

Combine ground meat, salt and pepper with the garlic and liquid smoke. Mix and then place the ground meat on wax paper and shape into four large patties. Make them a bit larger than usual as they will be stuffed. Next, stuff center of burgers with sliced cheese. Fold so that the cheese is covered and only meat remains on the outside. Broil in a preheated oven approximately 12 minutes. Serve hot on a bun with your favorite additions.

Alan McCall and his grandson Benjamin McCall
Tallahassee
WDXD/Big D Country

Turkey Tetrazzini

Everyone loves this dish; I make it often.

2 cups cubed cooked turkey
1 (8-ounce) package spaghetti, prepared per package directions
1 (8-ounce) can sliced mushrooms, drained
2 (10.75-ounce) cans cream of chicken (or cream of mushroom) soup
1 (16-ounce) container sour cream
1 cup frozen green peas
Parmesan cheese

Combine all ingredients except cheese; pour into a 9x13-inch baking dish. Sprinkle heavily with Parmesan. Bake at 350° for 45 minutes. (Can be frozen before cooking. Just thaw and cook.) Serves 8.

Sue Dannahower, Fort Pierce

Fish & Seafood

Jupiter Inlet Lighthouse

Uncle Charles' Baked Fish

Uncle Charles grew up around Saint Teresa and Alligator Point, fishing and taking advantage of the variety of seafood in the area. His baked fish recipe is a fantastic alternative to typical fried fillets.

Olive oil
1 cup chopped onion
½ cup chopped bell pepper
1 cup diced tomatoes
4 large whitefish fillets
1 teaspoon salt
½ teaspoon black pepper
1 tablespoon Worcestershire sauce
1 stick butter
1 cup grated Parmesan cheese

Preheat oven to 350°. Prepare a glass baking dish with olive oil and spread onion, bell pepper and tomatoes across bottom. Place fillets on top and season with salt, pepper and Worcestershire. Dot with butter and bake 8 to 10 minutes. Remove from oven and baste fish with drippings; cook an additional 6 to 8 minutes. Top with Parmesan and broil just until cheese melts. Serve hot.

Charles Johnson, Tallahassee

Coconut-Encrusted Mahi with Plantains & Pineapple

1 cup breadcrumbs
1 cup unsweetened coconut flakes
4 mahi fillets
2 eggs, beaten
6 tablespoons butter, divided
2 very ripe plantains, peeled and sliced
4 slices pineapple, cubed

Combine breadcrumbs and coconut flakes in a bowl. Dip fillets in egg; dredge in breadcrumb mixture. Fry in 4 tablespoons butter in a hot skillet until golden brown on both sides and cooked through, 2 to 3 minutes per side. Melt remaining 2 tablespoons butter in a separate skillet. Cook plantains with pineapple until browned on the edges and golden all over. Serve Mahi hot topped with plantains and pineapple.

Nicole Nolan, Islamorada

Florida Seafood Festival

Battery Park • 1st Weekend in November

The Florida Seafood Festival is a two-day event, annually drawing tens of thousands of visitors to the historic town of Apalachicola in scenic Franklin County. The Festival is held at the mouth of the Apalachicola River under the shady oaks of Apalachicola's Battery Park. The festival features delicious seafood, arts and crafts exhibits, seafood-related events, and musical entertainment. Some of the notable events include oyster eating and oyster shucking contests, blue crab races, photo contest, parade, 5k redfish run, the blessing of the fleet, history of the festival exhibit, and tonging for treasure.

1 Bay Avenue • Apalachicola, FL 32320
850.653.4720 • www.floridaseafoodfestival.com
Facebook: floridaseafoodfestival

Cornmeal-Crusted Lionfish with Caramelized Mango & Onions

Lionfish is an invasive species in the Atlantic, Gulf of Mexico, and Caribbean waters. They have no natural enemies. They are, however, excellent to eat once you remove the venomous spines. If lionfish is not available, a good substitute is hogfish or grouper.

½ pound lionfish fillets
¼ cup fresh-squeezed lime juice
¼ cup yellow cornmeal
½ teaspoon Montreal chicken seasoning
⅛ teaspoon ground black pepper
2 tablespoons butter, divided
1 tablespoon canola oil
¼ cup chopped onion
½ cup cubed mango
⅛ teaspoon kosher salt
2 tablespoons white wine

Prepare lionfish by sprinkling with lime juice. Combine cornmeal, chicken seasoning and black pepper in a zip-close food bag. Add fish and coat evenly. Melt 1 tablespoon butter with oil in a sauté pan over medium heat. Sauté fish until golden brown or till it flakes with a fork. Do not overcook. Set aside in a warm place while you prepare caramelized mango and onion using the same skillet. Add last tablespoon of butter to pan along with onion, mango and salt. Sauté until they start to caramelize then add wine to deglaze. Plate lionfish topped with mango and onions.

Chef Eileen Morris, Crystal Beach
www.personalcheftampabay.com

Florida Grouper with Roasted Vegetables

1 large Florida grouper fillet (approximately 1 pound)
3 tablespoons olive oil, divided
1 lemon
Freshly ground black pepper
1 teaspoon dried oregano
¾ teaspoon dried sweet basil
1 teaspoon kosher salt
1 small Florida zucchini, chopped into thin rounds
1 Florida carrot, chopped into small rounds
½ red Florida bell pepper, chopped
½ yellow Florida bell pepper, chopped
1 medium Florida onion, chopped
8 Florida cherry tomatoes, quartered
1 tablespoon ketchup
1½ cups tomato juice
1 tablespoon brown or natural sugar

Preheat oven to 350°. Place cleaned fish in middle of a baking pan. Spread 1 tablespoon olive oil over fish, making sure to cover both sides. Squeeze lemon juice on both sides and sprinkle with black pepper to taste. In a small cup, mix oregano, basil and salt, and sprinkle over both sides of fish. Set aside. Sauté chopped vegetables in remaining olive oil over medium heat just enough to soften a little. Pour over fish. In a bowl, mix ketchup, tomato juice and sugar; pour over fish. Cover and baked until done (flesh should be soft and flaky). Do not overcook. A general rule for cooking fish is 10 minutes per inch of thickness.

www.freshfromflorida.com

Grilled Catfish with Coffee Butter

1 tablespoon lemon juice
1 tablespoon instant coffee powder
¼ cup melted butter
2 teaspoons Pirate Jonny's Caribbean Roundup seasoning
¼ teaspoon onion powder
½ teaspoon salt
2 pounds catfish fillets

Combine lemon juice, instant coffee, butter, Caribbean seasoning, onion powder and salt. Brush thickly onto fillets. Broil 10 minutes. Turn and brush fish again with Coffee Butter. Broil 10 minutes longer or until fish flakes easily. Brush 1 last time with Coffee Butter and serve.

Terri and Jonathan Toner, Clearwater
Pirate Jonny's Caribbean Rubs & Seasonings

Clearwater Beach

Key Lime–Jalapeño Red Snapper Fillets

This recipe is made using our Key Limen Wine, named after a term our family and customers repeated often as we developed our Key Lime Wine over a decade. When time for yet another taste test, the question would be "What are you down?" Answer? "Key Limen!"

2 (8-ounce) red snapper fillets
¼ cup Key Limen wine
2 to 3 teaspoons olive oil
1 teaspoon chopped fresh parsley

6 cloves garlic, minced
1 large jalapeño pepper, chopped
2 tablespoons butter, melted

Arrange red snapper fillets in a single layer in a shallow dish. Whisk wine and olive oil in a bowl until blended. Stir in parsley, garlic, jalapeño and butter. Pour olive oil mixture over fillets tossing to coat. Let stand at room temperature 1 hour, turning occasionally. Preheat grill to high; reduce temperature to medium. Grill fillets until they flake easily.

Ray Shook, St. Petersburg
Florida Orange Groves Winery

Grilled Mango Chutney–Marinated Fish Fillets

4 tablespoons Jacquie's Jamming Special mango chutney
1 tablespoon lime juice
1 teaspoon grated fresh ginger
1 clove garlic, crushed
½ teaspoon ground cumin
½ teaspoon chopped fresh cilantro
Chili powder to taste
4 medium whitefish fillets

Combine all ingredients, except fish, as a marinade. Spread evenly over fish fillets—both sides. Refrigerate, covered, at least 20 minutes. Preheat grill and cook over medium-high heat, basting with remaining marinade as you grill. Grilling time will vary depending on how thick your fillets are and temperature of your grill. Fish will flake easily when cooked.

Jacquie Hoare-Ward, Naples
Jacquie's Jamming Jams

Tasha's Loaded Poke Bowl

This is one of my favorite things from the Food & Wine festival that I loved attending while working in Orlando and at Disney and Epcot as a photographer. Now I make the same dish on special occasions.

1½ cups white rice
1½ pounds sushi-grade ahi tuna
3 tablespoons low-sodium soy sauce
2 teaspoons toasted sesame oil
1 tablespoon rice wine vinegar
1 teaspoon grated ginger
1 teaspoon minced garlic
Chili paste
2 green scallions, white and green parts, thinly sliced
2 large, ripe avocados
½ cup grated baby carrots
1 bunch (about 8) medium radish, thinly sliced
Sesame seeds
1 bunch fresh cilantro, chopped

First, rinse rice in a fine-mesh strainer. Cook rice according to instructions on the packaging or the directions for your rice cooker. With a sharp knife, cut the ahi into 1-inch cubes. In a large bowl, whisk together soy sauce, sesame oil, vinegar, ginger, garlic and chili paste to taste. Add ahi and shallots and stir gently to combine. Keep chilled. Just before serving, pit and dice the avocado into small cubes. Arrange your poke bowl with a generous scoop of rice, ahi tuna, avocado, carrot and radish. Sprinkle sesame seeds on top. Serve with cilantro and more soy sauce on the side.

Tasha Koetsch, Orlando
Wanderlust Boudoir by TK Photographies

Triple Citrus Salmon

Glaze:

¾ cup fresh orange juice
¼ cup fresh lemon juice
¼ cup fresh lime juice
¼ cup chicken stock
1 clove garlic, minced
2 tablespoons orange marmalade
2 tablespoons soy sauce
1 tablespoon rice wine vinegar
1 tablespoon packed light brown sugar
1 tablespoon butter
Pinch salt and cracked black pepper

Bring all ingredients to a boil in a medium-size saucepan over medium heat, stirring to melt the marmalade and to keep the mixture from burning. Reduce heat to a simmer and reduce until syrupy, about 15 to 20 minutes. Adjust seasonings to taste.

Salmon:

4 (6-ounce) salmon fillets, 1 inch thick
Extra virgin olive oil for brushing
Salt and cracked black pepper

Heat a grill to medium-high heat. Brush both sides of fillets with olive oil just before grilling, then season with salt and pepper to taste. Grill salmon about 4 minutes per side, brushing with glaze during the final few minutes of cooking. Transfer salmon to serving plates and brush with remaining glaze before serving.

Cindy Walker, Lakeland

Nana's Salmon Patties

Lisa and I are about the same age and attended high school together. Our parents, and grandparents, would also be around the same age. This recipe is almost identical to my grandfather Angus Campbell's recipe for salmon patties which he shared with me from his recipe collection from World War II. It was designed to feed as many people as possible with as little as possible during war-time rationing. My mom often said when she was a child growing up in wartime, that she was never really sure if any salmon was ever included. "Daddy," she said, "could stretch a can of salmon juice over 3 or 4 tins of crackers." Amazing that a wartime rationing recipe has become a family favorite for so many.

—Kent Whitaker

1 (14.75-ounce) can pink salmon
1 egg, beaten
¼ (16-ounce) box saltine crackers, crumbled (1 sleeve crackers)
Butter-flavored Crisco for cooking

Empty salmon into a shallow bowl. Remove skin and bones, retaining liquid with the salmon. Flake salmon with a fork; add egg and stir well. Crush crackers in a separate shallow bowl. Using about 2 tablespoons salmon, roll it in cracker crumbs and form into a patty. Fry in a hot skillet using butter-flavored Crisco, turn and cook until golden brown on both sides. Drain and serve hot.

Lisa Barnes, Palm Beach

Sunshine Salmon Fillets

I make this recipe two ways—with a sweet white wine or with chicken stock. The wine version has a lighter, more summery feel where the chicken-stock version is heartier. Both are really good.

2 oranges, divided
½ cup sweet white wine or chicken stock
2 teaspoons finely chopped garlic
1 tablespoon finely chopped fresh dill
4 (6-ounce) salmon fillets, skin removed
¼ teaspoon black pepper
1 teaspoon salt-free garlic & herb seasoning
2 tablespoons orange marmalade
1 tablespoon Dijon mustard
1 tablespoon unsalted butter

Cut half an orange into ¼-inch-thick round slices; cut slices into quarters. Juice remaining oranges to make about ½ cup. Pour into a large sauté pan over medium-high heat. Add wine, garlic, dill and orange slices. Cover and bring a boil. Reduce heat to low; simmer, uncovered, 7 minutes. Check fillets for bones; season both sides with black pepper and garlic & herb seasoning. Add salmon to sauté pan and cook 3 to 4 minutes on each side. When done, fillets will flake easily with a fork. Remove from pan and plate the salmon. Working quickly, add marmalade and mustard to wine mixture; cook and stir about 1 minute or until marmalade dissolves and sauce thickens. Remove from heat and stir in butter. Pour sauce over salmon and serve.

Cindy Walker, Lakeland

Beer-Battered Shark Bites

1 pound shark fillets
Vegetable oil for frying
1½ cups flour plus additional flour for dredging
2 teaspoons garlic powder
1½ teaspoons onion powder
1 teaspoon paprika
1 teaspoon salt
1 teaspoon black pepper
Hot sauce to taste, optional
1 (12-ounce) can beer

Cube shark meat into bite-size pieces (no bigger than a quarter but bigger than a nickel). Heat oil in a stockpot or fryer. Combine 1½ cups flour and remaining ingredients in a large bowl; mix well. Place additional flour in a separate shallow bowl. Dredge shark bites in flour, then dip in batter to fully coat. Working in batches, frying in hot oil until golden brown. Drain on a rack or paper towels. Season to taste with additional seasonings. Serve hot.

Stephanie Owler Loudermilk, Titusville

Uncle Charles' Shrimp & Beer

1 medium onion, chopped
1 clove garlic, crushed
3 tablespoons oil
2 pounds shrimp, peeled and deveined
1 teaspoon salt
½ teaspoon black pepper
2 tablespoons chopped parsley
½ teaspoon celery seed
1 (16-ounce) can beer

In a large skillet over medium-high heat, sauté onion and garlic in oil 2 to 3 minutes. Add shrimp; stir then add remaining ingredients. Simmer 8 to 10 minutes.

Charles Johnson, Tallahassee

Beer-Boiled Shrimp & Ramen Noodles

This is an easy recipe. When the kids and I were in Pensacola Beach, times were tough. I would make a point to meet up with a nice gentleman who drove "the shrimp truck from Apalachicola" because he had the biggest, best, and least expensive shrimp. We always stopped at Winn-Dixie for an ice-cold Coke—25 cents out of the machine. He loved that we stopped to get him something to cool off with and always gave us a deal. We would get a pound of shrimp for next to nothing, take it home and I would stir-fry them on a hot plate with whatever beer my dad left in the fridge. Tough times make good memories and interesting recipes.

1 pound shrimp, beheaded and cleaned
1 (12-ounce) can beer
Salt and pepper to taste
2 (3-ounce) packages ramen noodles
1 (14.5-ounce) can peas and carrots, drained

Cook shrimp in skillet with your favorite beer over medium heat until they turn pink—no more than 3 minutes or they will become tough. Cook noodles per package directions; stir in peas and carrots. Serve shrimp over noodles and vegetables.

Christine Morgan, Pensacola and Panama City

Buffalo Shrimp

If you like Buffalo wings but don't like the calories from the fried Buffalo wings (chicken), this is a great substitute.

- 1 cup hot sauce
- 2 teaspoons dry yellow mustard
- 2 teaspoons cayenne pepper
- ½ (10-ounce) bottle Tiger sauce
- ¾ cup Tabasco sauce
- ½ teaspoon crushed red pepper flakes
- 2 tablespoons sugar
- 3 pounds shrimp, shells on
- 1 (16-ounce) bottle blue cheese dressing
- Carrot sticks
- Celery sticks

In a large pot, mix together 2 cups water, hot sauce, mustard, cayenne pepper, Tiger sauce, Tabasco, red pepper flakes and sugar; bring to a boil. Add shrimp; boil 2 minutes. Remove from heat; chill shrimp in brine. The longer they remain in brine, the hotter they become. Drain shrimp. Serve with blue cheese dressing, carrot sticks and celery sticks. Serves 8 to 10.

Sue Dannahower, Fort Pierce

Key Lime-Chili Shrimp

- 1½ pounds medium deveined Key West pink shrimp (about 6 per person)
- 2 tablespoons Pirate Jonny's Key-Lime Chili seasoning
- 2 tablespoons melted butter
- 2 tablespoons extra virgin olive oil
- Sliced onion, large pieces for skewers
- Sliced bell pepper, large pieces for skewers

Mix all ingredients together, place in zip-close bag and marinate no more than 15 minutes. Place on skewers and grill (or broil) 2 minutes per side. Serve with couscous or rice. Dust with PJ's Key Lime-Chili seasoning just before serving, if desired.

Terri and Jonathan Toner, Clearwater
Pirate Jonny's Caribbean Rubs & Seasonings

Catur's Cajun Shrimp Pronto

This recipe is very easy and tastes fantastic served with white rice, yellow, or even wild rice.

- 2 tablespoons vegetable oil
- 1 cup chopped onion
- 1 cup finely chopped celery
- ½ cup finely chopped green bell pepper
- ½ cup finely chopped red bell pepper
- 2 cloves garlic, minced
- 2 cups chopped peeled tomatoes
- 1 (8-ounce) can tomato sauce
- 1 pound uncooked shrimp, peeled and deveined
- ¾ tablespoon Cajun seasoning
- ½ teaspoon freshly ground black pepper
- ½ teaspoon hot sauce
- ⅓ cup cooking wine
- 4 cups hot cooked rice

Heat oil in a large saucepan over medium-high heat. Add onion, celery, bell peppers and garlic; cook 3 to 5 minutes or until soft. Add tomatoes and tomato sauce; cook an additional 5 minutes. Add shrimp, seasoning, hot sauce and wine. Cook another 5 minutes just until shrimp turn pink (careful not to overcook). Serve over rice.

Catur Turnbull, Green Cove Springs
United States Navy

Honey Italian Grilled Shrimp

This is my tried-and-true method for grilling shrimp; it never fails.

2 pounds uncooked medium to large shrimp, peeled and deveined
1 cup Italian salad dressing
½ tablespoon Italian seasoning
¾ cup honey
2 teaspoons garlic powder
½ tablespoon cooking oil

Place shrimp in a zip-close bag. Combine remaining ingredients. Pour half in bag with shrimp; reserve the remainder for basting. Turn bag to evenly coat shrimp. Refrigerate at least 1 hour. When ready to cook; prepare grill to medium heat. Drain shrimp and discard marinade. Thread shrimp onto 8 skewers. (If they are really big shrimp, use 2 skewers for each with a bit of space between. This keeps the shrimp from spinning.) Grill over medium heat, basting frequently. Cook about 4 minutes per side or until shrimp is done and have nice golden-brown edges.

Catur Turnbull, Green Cove Springs
United States Navy

Fried Shrimp

When growing up, if I heard the sound of oil crackling in the kitchen, I knew my dad was making his classic Fried Shrimp. It's absolutely delicious and continues to be a staple around our family dinner table.

Shrimp Sauce:
- ⅔ cup mayonnaise
- ⅓ cup ketchup
- ½ teaspoon Datil pepper sauce
- Dash Tabasco sauce

Combine ingredients in a small bowl; refrigerate until ready to serve.

Shrimp:
- 6 pounds large raw shrimp (average ½ pound per person)
- 3 eggs
- Salt, pepper and paprika
- 1 (10-ounce) package cracker meal
- 1 pound vegetable oil shortening for deep frying

Peel shrimp leaving tail on. Devein and split to first tail joint; set aside. Beat eggs; season to taste. Place meal in a shallow bowl and season to taste. Dip shrimp into eggs; roll in cracker meal. Fry in hot oil until golden brown. Drain on brown paper bag. Serve hot with Shrimp Sauce.

John Cox, professional bass angler, DeBary

"Jolly Mon" Grilled Shrimp

1 tablespoon packed brown sugar
1 tablespoon Italian seasoning
1 tablespoon salt
2 teaspoons black pepper
1 teaspoon ground allspice
1 teaspoon ground cinnamon
1 teaspoon granulated garlic
1 teaspoon granulated ginger
1 teaspoon Sazon Goya (coriander and annatto seasoning)
½ teaspoon ground cayenne pepper
½ teaspoon ground turmeric
¼ teaspoon ground nutmeg
24 large raw shrimp, peeled and deveined
Canola oil spray
1 lime, quartered

Soak 4 wooden skewers in water 1 hour. Combine sugar and all spices in a covered container to make spice dust. (This makes more than you need so you will have extra for the next time you cook this recipe—and you probably will.) Preheat barbecue grill to medium high. Thread 6 shrimp on each skewer, piercing each twice to form a C shape. Stack shrimp so they all lay flat when placed on grill. Spray shrimp lightly on both sides with canola oil; dust with spices. (More dust = more flavor, salt and heat.) Place shrimp skewers on grill; move them slightly after 30 seconds to prevent sticking. Grill until toasty brown; turn and do the same with other side. It will only take about 3 to 4 minutes per side; do not overcook. Remove shrimp from heat; drizzle with lime juice. Serve immediately.

Karl Mrozek, Fernandina Beach
Nassau Sport Fishing Association

Fried Green Tomatoes with Sautéed Shrimp–Corn Machoux over Cheesy Grits with Andouille Gravy

Shrimp–Corn Machoux:
32 shrimp, peeled, shells reserved
4 ears corn, shucked and kernels removed
½ onion, chopped
½ red bell pepper, chopped
2 ribs celery, chopped
2 tablespoons butter
12 grape tomatoes, halved
1 bunch green onion tops, finely sliced

Make a shrimp stock by combining 4 cups water, shrimp shells and trimmings from celery and onion in a saucepan. Bring to a boil; simmer 45 minutes. Strain; reduce liquid to 1 cup. Sauté corn, onion, bell pepper and celery in butter 5 minutes; add shrimp, sauté until done. Add tomatoes; stir to warm through.

Andouille Gravy:
2 tablespoons butter
2 poblano peppers, coarsely chopped
1 jalapeño, finely chopped
1 clove garlic, minced
1 cup shrimp stock
1 cup heavy cream
4 ounces andouille sausage, finely minced
½ cup grated Parmesan cheese

Sauté poblano peppers, jalapeño and garlic in butter until tender. Add stock, cream, andouille and Parmesan. Bring to a boil; simmer until ready to serve.

Grits:
1 cup Anson Mills grits
3 cups water
1 cup heavy cream
1 (8-ounce) block Cheddar cheese, shredded

Prepare grits as per instructions. (The amounts of water and cream given are for Anson Mills. They will take about 1 hour to prepare.) When cooked stir in cheese until melted and blended.

Fried Green Tomatoes:
8 slices green tomatoes, ¼ inch thick
Yellow cornmeal
Egg wash
Oil for frying

Dredge tomatoes in cornmeal, then egg wash, and then cornmeal; dredge in egg and cornmeal a third time. Sauté or fry until golden and crispy. To serve, ladle a quarter of the grits onto each of 4 plates; place 2 fried green tomatoes on each plate. Equally distribute Shrimp–Corn Machoux over grits. Spoon or drizzle Andouille Gravy around plate; garnish with green onions. Serves 4.

Isle of Eight Flags Shrimp Festival & Pirate Parade
Chef Brian Grimley at Lulu's at the Thompson House
Fernandina Beach

Isle of Eight Flags Shrimp Festival & Pirate Parade

Fernandina Beach • 1st Weekend in May

This delicious northeast Florida tradition, presented by Baptist Medical Center–Nassau, kicks-off with a Pirate Parade in downtown Fernandina Beach. The festival officially opens Friday afternoon with a Kids' Fun Zone, food booths, a pageant, live music, fireworks, a pirate invasion, and more. The festival continues Saturday and Sunday with two stages; nearly 400 vendors displaying fine arts, crafts and antiques, contests; children's activities; nationally recognized entertainers; and lots of shrimp! Learn more at ShrimpFestival.com

Historic Downtown Fernandina Beach
Fernandina Beach, FL 32034
904.583.0659 • www.shrimpfestival.com

Sabrina's Book Club Shrimp & Sausage

1 pound Cajun andouille sausage, sliced or butterflied
4 dozen jumbo Florida wild-caught shrimp, peeled, deveined and butterflied
2 tablespoons olive oil
Captain Mike's seasoning
½ cup shredded Cheddar cheese

Preheat oven to 400°. Arrange sausage on a nonstick baking pan. Bake 5 minutes. Remove pan and add shrimp, making sure butterfly cuts are open. Drizzle olive oil over shrimp and sausage. Evenly sprinkle with Captain Mike's seasoning. Cook 4 minutes. Top with cheese and return to oven just until cheese is melted and bubbly.

Sabrina Bethurum, Satellite Beach

Dania Beach Arts & Seafood Celebration

Dania Beach • May

Don't miss out on a fun-filled weekend at the Dania Beach Arts & Seafood Celebration. Bring your appetites to feast on an array of delicious seafood and specialty treats as you groove to live entertainment all weekend long. Experience hands-on arts and crafts while admiring and purchasing your favorite creations from artist vendors. Witness local artists paint masterpieces during live street art performances. Kids can enjoy exciting and fun activities at Dania Beach Kids Funville while watching the 100-ton sandcastle come to life. Plus, get ready for a tasty competition at the Chef Showcase. Admission and parking are free.

Frost Park • 300 NE 2nd Street • Dania Beach, FL 33004
954.924.6801 • www.daniabeachartsandseafoodcelebration.com
Facebook: DaniaBeachArtsandSeafoodCelebration

Shrimp Scampi & Pasta

1½ pounds fresh shrimp, beheaded and peeled
4 to 5 cloves garlic, minced
4 tablespoons olive oil, divided
½ cup chopped green onion
4 Roma tomatoes, cut into 1-inch pieces
1 (8-ounce) package pasta
2 teaspoons extra virgin olive oil
Kosher salt
Freshly ground black pepper, optional
Chopped fresh parsley, optional

In a bowl, toss shrimp with minced garlic and 2 tablespoons olive oil; set aside. In a sauté pan over medium heat, sauté green onion in remaining 2 tablespoons olive oil until transparent. Add shrimp and cook until shrimp are pink, about 4 minutes (don't overcook). Add tomatoes, give it a stir, and remove from heat. Cook pasta in salted water to al dente per package directions; drain reserving 1 cup pasta water. Add ¼ cup pasta water and 2 teaspoons extra virgin olive oil to pasta pot; return to a boil. Transfer drained pasta back to pot. Carefully spoon shrimp mixture into pot with pasta. Gently toss to combine, adding some pasta water 2 tablespoons at a time until desired consistency is achieved. Salt to taste. Transfer to plates; sprinkle with pepper or fresh parsley if desired.

Isle of Eight Flags Shrimp Festival & Pirate Parade

Shrimp Arnaud

6 tablespoons olive oil
2 tablespoons wine vinegar
3 teaspoons horseradish mustard
1½ teaspoons paprika
1½ tablespoons chopped scallion tops
4 tablespoons chopped celery
1 tablespoon chopped fresh parsley
1 tablespoon grated onion
2 pounds boiled shrimp, shelled and deveined
Shredded lettuce
Salt and pepper to taste

In a large bowl, make sauce by combining olive oil, vinegar, mustard, paprika, scallion tops, celery, parsley and onion; mix well. Add shrimp and refrigerate at least 2 hours to marinate. Serve on shredded lettuce. Season with salt and pepper. Serves 6.

Sue Dannahower, Fort Pierce

Florida Orange Groves Crab Cakes

1 pound Alaskan king crabmeat
⅓ cup breadcrumbs
¼ cup mayonnaise
1 egg, beaten
1 teaspoon Worcestershire sauce
1 teaspoon dry mustard
1 teaspoon minced parsley
1 teaspoon salt
1 teaspoon white pepper
2 ounces Florida pink grapefruit wine

Combined crabmeat, breadcrumbs, mayonnaise, egg, Worcestershire, dry mustard, parsley, salt, pepper and Florida grapefruit wine. Form into individual crab cakes. Bake at 350° until lightly browned.

Vince Shook, St. Petersburg
Florida Orange Groves Winery

St. Petersburg

Crab Puffs

1 (8-ounce) can crabmeat, drained and flaked
½ cup shredded sharp Cheddar cheese
3 green onions, chopped
1 teaspoon Worcestershire sauce
½ teaspoon dry mustard
1 tablespoon hot sauce
1 stick butter
¼ teaspoon salt
1 cup flour
4 eggs
¼ cup sour cream
2 tablespoons horseradish
2 tablespoons mayonnaise
Salt and pepper

Preheat oven to 400°. Combine crabmeat, cheese, onions, Worcestershire, dry mustard and hot sauce in a bowl; mix well. Add butter and salt to large saucepan over medium-high heat. Add 1 cup water and bring to a boil. Remove from heat and immediately add flour, beating until mixture leaves the sides of the pan and forms a ball. Add eggs, 1 at a time, beating thoroughly after each addition. Thoroughly blend in crab mixture. Drop by small teaspoon-size pieces onto a greased baking sheet. Bake 15 to 20 minutes. Combine sour cream, horseradish and mayonnaise to make a dipping sauce; season with salt and pepper. Serve Crab Puffs warm with dipping sauce on the side.

Uncle Charles and Aunt Wynona Johnson, Tallahassee

Grilled Spiny Lobster Tails with Garlic Butter Dipping Sauce

1½ teaspoons seafood seasoning
4 whole spiny lobster tails
1 tablespoon minced garlic

Dash salt and pepper
Lemon juice

Bring a pot of water large enough to hold all 4 tails to a boil; add seafood seasoning. Lower heat to simmer. Add tails and cook 2 to 3 minutes. Working quickly and using heat resistant gloves, remove tails. Use a sharp knife or kitchen shears to cut open shell, cut meat and fold back. Top with garlic, salt and pepper to taste. Place on a hot grill and cook until meat has completely turned white and shell has grill marks. Top with lemon juice after removing from heat. Serve hot with Garlic Butter Dipping Sauce.

Garlic Butter Dipping Sauce:

1½ sticks butter, melted
1 to 2 teaspoons minced garlic

Dash parsley flakes
Dash salt

Combine all ingredients in a bowl.

Paul Siverson, Titusville

Deering Seafood Festival

Oviedo • Last Weekend in May

Get ready for a nonstop celebration at the Deering Seafood Festival, complete with delicious catches from the sea, celebrity chef cooking demos, fun-filled adventures for kids, Virgin Island stilt walkers, a Bahamian Junkanoo musical parade, and on-going live entertainment. Area restaurants and caterers line Seafood Alley, while acclaimed chefs host cooking demonstrations under the big top tent. Don't miss Discovery Cove, where kids can experiment and explore; Shrimp Kids Zone, with fun activities and healthy tastings and recipes for families; unlimited play on inflatables; and a kid-friendly menu. Other activities include Pelican Skipper pontoon boat rides, nature tours, and Artist Lane.

16701 SW 72nd Avenue • Miami, FL 33157
305.235.1668 ext. 263 • www.deeringestate.org
Facebook: deeringestate

Broiled Lobster Tail & Hogfish Fillets

I spearfish all of the time and love to eat seafood. This is my foolproof recipe for cooking lobster tail and fish fillets. Fast and yummy.

2 lobster tails
2 hogfish fillets
1 lemon, juiced
2 cloves garlic, minced
Basil, salt and pepper

Preheat oven to broil. Cut top of lobster tail shell with kitchen scissors; open gently to expose meat. Arrange both tails and both fillets on a nonstick baking sheet; drizzle lightly with lemon juice. Top each with a small amount of minced garlic; sprinkle with basil, salt and pepper to taste. Broil 9 to 10 minutes or until fish flakes easily.

Heather Kirby, Fort Lauderdale

Fellsmere Frog Leg Festival

Fellsmere • 3rd Thursday in January

The Fellsmere Frog Leg Festival has been a local favorite over twenty-five years and truly has something for every member of your family. Whether you're joining us for the famous mouthwatering frog leg and gator tail dinners, or to browse the hundreds of booths for unique gifts, or to listen to some great music and enjoy the fun rides, you'll immediately know why this festival has become a success and an annual tradition for so many. Fellsmere has been proclaimed Frog Leg Capital of the World, and The Frog Leg Festival holds two Guinness world records: the most frog legs served in the course of one business day and the largest frog leg festival in the world. With over 80,000 attendees enjoying over 7,000 pounds of frog legs and 2,000 pounds of gator, the Frog Leg Festival has come a long way from its humble roots.

22 South Orange Street • Fellsmere, FL 32948
772-571-0250 • www.froglegfestival.com
Facebook: fellsmerefroglegfestival

Frog Legs

8 ounces fresh frog legs
2 cups flour
1 cup cornmeal
1 teaspoon salt
1 teaspoon pepper
½ teaspoon garlic powder
Pinch cayenne pepper
1 cup vegetable oil

Dry frog legs completely. Mix flour, cornmeal, salt, pepper, garlic powder and cayenne until combined. Toss frog legs in flour mixture until coated. In a deep skillet, heat vegetable oil to 350°. Add frog legs; cook 5 to 7 minutes or until golden brown.

Fellsmere Frog Leg Festival, Fellsmere

Oysters Rockefeller

36 live oysters
2 cups cooked spinach
4 tablespoons chopped onion
2 bay leaves
1 tablespoon chopped fresh parsley
½ teaspoon celery salt
½ teaspoon salt
6 drops hot pepper sauce
6 tablespoons butter or margarine
½ cup breadcrumbs
Lemon slices for garnish

Preheat oven to 400°. Shuck oysters (reserve 36 shells) and rinse in cold water. Combine spinach, onion, bay leaves and parsley in a food processor. Pulse to mix. Add celery salt, salt and hot sauce; pulse to mix. Cook with butter in a saucepan over medium heat 5 minutes. Add breadcrumbs and mix well. Spread mixture over oyster meat in shells and bake 10 minutes. Serve hot garnished with lemon slices.

Lisa Barnes, Palm Beach

Titusville • 1st Weekend in April

The Titusville Strawberry Fest celebrates strawberries in all their berry goodness. Kids will enjoy pony rides, train rides, bounce houses, a petting farm, a hula hoop contest, and more. Don't miss out on tasty strawberry shortcake and chocolate-covered strawberries. Visitors may also take home fresh strawberries to enjoy. The event also features live music, so you can dance all weekend long.

Sand Point Park • 101 North Washington Avenue • Titusville, FL 32796
386.860.0092 • www.TitusvilleFest.com
Facebook: TitusvilleStrawberryFest

Cakes

Everglades National Park

Florida Orange Fruitcake

6 oranges
¾ cup butter, softened
2½ cups sugar, divided
3 eggs
3 cups flour plus additional as needed
1½ teaspoons baking soda
1 cup buttermilk
1½ cups chopped dates
1 cup chopped pecans

Preheat oven to 350°. Zest 1 orange to get 1 tablespoon zest. Juice all oranges to extract 1½ cups plus 1 tablespoon orange juice; set aside. Cream butter and 1½ cups sugar; add eggs and mix until fluffy. Add orange zest and 1 tablespoon juice. In a separate bowl, sift flour and baking soda; add to orange mixture alternately with buttermilk. Flour dates and nuts and fold into cake mixture. Pour into a greased and floured 10x14-inch pan, or divide and pour into 2 small greased and floured bread pans. Bake 1 hour. While cake is baking, make an orange syrup by stirring remaining 1 cup sugar into reserved 1½ cups orange juice; mix thoroughly. Turn cake out of pan, bottom side up. Slowly spread orange syrup over cake until it is all soaked in.

Suncoast BBQ & Bluegrass Bash

Venice • March

Suncoast BBQ & Bluegrass Bash is southwest Florida's largest BBQ and bluegrass event. The festival features the nation's top pit masters as well as the best bluegrass bands in the land. Admission, parking, and entertainment are free at this family-friendly, finger-lickin', and hot-pickin' good time.

610 Airport Avenue East • Venice, FL 34285
941.809.5232 • www.suncoastbbqbash.com
Facebook: SuncoastBBQBash

Orange Cream Cake

Cake:
1¾ cups sifted cake flour
1 tablespoon baking powder
¼ teaspoon salt
½ cup shortening
1 cup sugar
8 egg yolks, beaten
1 teaspoon grated orange rind
½ cup milk

Preheat oven to 350°. Have all ingredients at room temperature. Sift together flour, baking powder and salt; sift again and set aside. Cream shortening till fluffy; gradually add sugar beating well. Beat in egg yolks and orange rind until well mixed. Alternately add dry ingredients and milk, beating after each addition. Turn into 2 greased 8-inch cake pans and bake 30 minutes. Cool 5 minutes in pan; turn onto cooling rack. When cooled, fill with Orange Rum Filling and frost with whipped cream.

Orange Rum Filling:
3 tablespoons butter, softened
¾ teaspoon grated orange rind
1½ cups sifted powdered sugar, divided
Salt
2 tablespoons orange juice
1 teaspoon rum
1 (12-ounce) container whipped topping

Cream butter with grated orange rind. Gradually add ½ cup powdered sugar, blending well. Add dash of salt; mix well. Add remaining 1 cup powdered sugar alternately with orange juice, beating till smooth after each addition. Blend in rum. Spread between cake layers. Frost top and sides with whipped topping.

Sunshine Cake

Cake:
- **1 box yellow cake mix**
- **¼ cup applesauce**
- **4 eggs**
- **1 (11-ounce) can Mandarin oranges in light syrup**

Preheat oven to 350°. Combine Cake ingredients in a large bowl; beat by hand 2 minutes. Coat a 9x13-inch pan with nonstick spray. Pour batter into pan. Bake 30 to 40 minutes or until a toothpick inserted in center comes out clean. Cool completely.

Frosting:
- **1 (8-ounce) container whipped topping**
- **1 (3-ounce) box instant vanilla pudding**
- **1 (20-ounce) can crushed pineapple, drained**

In a large bowl, combine Frosting ingredients until well blended. Spread over cake. Refrigerate until ready to serve; refrigerate leftovers.

Lemonade Cake

1 (3-ounce) package lemon gelatin
¾ cup boiling water
4 eggs
¾ cup cooking oil
1 box yellow cake mix
1 (6-ounce) can lemonade concentrate
½ cup sugar

Preheat oven to 350°. Dissolve lemon gelatin in boiling water; cool. Using an electric mixer, beat eggs thoroughly. Add cooking oil, cake mix and gelatin; mix well. Pour into a greased tube pan. Bake 1 hour or until a toothpick in center comes out clean. While cake bakes, make glaze by heating lemon concentrate in a small saucepan over medium heat. Add sugar and stir just until dissolved; remove from heat. When cake is done, remove from oven, leaving in tube pan. Drizzle with glaze; leave in pan 1 hour before removing.

Blueberry Cake

This Blueberry Cake recipe is my preferred stand-by dessert in case we are invited to a friend's house for dinner because it is quick and easy, uses ingredients I usually have on hand, yet makes an impressive presentation. Try it; you'll love it, too.

1 box yellow cake mix plus ingredients to prepare
1 (8-ounce) package cream cheese, softened
1 (8-ounce) container Cool Whip
1 (21-ounce) can blueberry pie filling

Prepare cake mix in 3 (8-inch) layers according to directions on box; cool. Combine cream cheese and three quarters of the Cool Whip. Place first cake layer on serving platter and cover with half the cream cheese mixture; top with half the blueberry pie filling. Place second layer on top. Cover with remaining cream cheese mixture and all but about 3 tablespoons of remaining pie filling. Place third layer on top; cover with remaining Cool Whip; decorate center with remaining pie filling.

Key Lime Pudding Cake

8 to 10 Key limes
¾ cup sugar
¼ cup all-purpose flour
Dash salt
3 tablespoons margarine, melted
3 eggs
1½ cups milk

Zest 1 Key lime to get ¼ teaspoon zest; set aside. Microwave limes 30 seconds to soften so they are easier to juice. Use a citrus reamer (or even just a fork) to extract ¼ cup juice; set aside. (Don't try to squeeze those small Key limes with your hands—you'll be miserable.) Preheat oven to 350°. In a bowl, combine sugar, flour and salt. Add melted margarine, lime zest and juice; mix well. Set aside. Separate eggs into 2 bowls, being careful not to get any yolk in the whites. Beat egg yolks and stir into cake batter. Add milk and mix well. In glass bowl using an electric mixer, beat egg whites until stiff. Fold gently into cake batter. Pour batter into a greased 8x8-inch baking pan. Pour hot water into a large, shallow baking pan to a depth of 1 inch. Set pan of pudding batter into hot water. Bake 40 minutes or until lightly browned. Serve warm or chilled, topping with whipped cream or softened vanilla ice cream. Serves 6.

Joy's Key Lime Gingerbread

Gingerbread dates back to the Middle Ages and is popular around the world. No longer made with stale bread and spices, today it's the molasses that makes it sweet and moist. In this version that my family loves so much, a Key Lime Hard Sauce makes it even more delicious.

Gingerbread:

- 1 stick (½ cup) butter, softened
- ½ cup firmly packed dark brown sugar
- 1 egg, beaten
- 2 cups flour
- 2 teaspoons baking powder
- ½ teaspoon baking soda
- 2 teaspoons ground ginger
- 1 teaspoon ground cinnamon
- ½ teaspoon ground cloves (or black pepper)
- ½ teaspoon salt
- ½ cup dark molasses
- ¾ cup buttermilk
- Candied ginger for garnish

Heat oven to 350°. With an electric mixer, using a large bowl, cream butter and sugar. (Leavening: this creates tiny air pockets around the sugar molecules.) Beat in egg (beaten egg incorporates air into what is to become a thick batter). In another bowl, whisk together flour, baking powder, baking soda, ginger, cinnamon, cloves and salt; set aside. (Whisking reduces lumps and combines ingredients to evenly add to batter.) In a small bowl, combine molasses and buttermilk; stir into creamed mixture then beat well. (Molasses and buttermilk act as an acid and will later react with the alkali baking soda; liquid ingredients activate it to produce a carbon dioxide gas for leavening.) Add dry ingredients and mix well; beat on medium speed 2½ minutes. Scrape batter into greased and floured 9x9-inch pan. Bake 45 minutes. Remove from oven and cool. When completely cooled, serve topped with Key Lime Hard Sauce and candied ginger.

Key Lime Hard Sauce:

- ½ cup butter, softened
- 1 tablespoon Key lime juice
- 1½ cups powdered sugar

Beat butter with lime juice until creamy. Gradually beat in powdered sugar, beating until light and fluffy.

Joy Harris, Tampa
www.joyharriscooks.com

Oatmeal-Coconut Cake

Oatmeal Cake:

1½ cups boiling water
1 cup quick-cooking rolled oats
1½ cups sifted all-purpose flour
1 teaspoon baking soda
1 teaspoon salt
1 teaspoon ground cinnamon

½ teaspoon baking powder
½ cup butter, softened
1 cup sugar
1 cup firmly packed light brown sugar
2 large eggs

Coconut Topping:

1⅓ cups flaked coconut
¼ cup butter, melted
½ cup firmly packed brown sugar

¼ cup heavy cream
1 teaspoon vanilla extract

Preheat oven to 350°. Combine boiling water and oats; set aside. Sift together flour, baking soda, salt, cinnamon and baking powder; set aside. With an electric mixer, beat butter and both sugars at medium speed until mealy; add eggs, 1 at a time, beating until light and fluffy. Stir in oats; add flour mixture, beating well. Pour batter into a greased and floured 9-inch-square pan. Bake 40 minutes; cool in pan 10 minutes. Transfer cake to a baking sheet. Combine Coconut Topping ingredients and spread over cake. Broil 2 to 3 minutes or until topping is lightly browned.

Dreamy Creamy Pineapple Cake

1 box pineapple cake mix plus ingredients to prepare
1 (16-ounce) can crushed pineapple, drained
1 (3-ounce) box instant French vanilla pudding
1 (8-ounce) package cream cheese, softened
1 (8-ounce) container Cool Whip

Bake cake in 9x13-inch glass dish per instructions on box (I like to use the drained pineapple juice as a portion of the liquid). When cake is cooked, remove from oven and poke holes in the top with a fork. Spread drained pineapple over cake while hot. In a medium-size bowl, prepare pudding according to directions on box. Add cream cheese; mix well. Pour this mixture evenly over cake. Top with Cool Whip. Keep refrigerated.

Coconut Sheet Cake

1 box moist white cake mix plus ingredients to prepare
1 teaspoon vanilla extract
1 (15-ounce) can cream of coconut
1 (14-ounce) can sweetened condensed milk
1 (8-ounce) container whipped cream
Coconut flakes

Prepare cake mix according to package directions; add vanilla before baking in a 9x13-inch pan. When a toothpick inserted in the center comes out clean, remove cake and poke holes in it with the handle of a wooden spoon. Mix cream of coconut and condensed milk together and pour over hot cake. Cool completely. Top with the whipped cream and coconut flakes.

Sue "Miss Sue" Young

Florida Strawberry Festival

Plant City • End of February or 1st of March

With nearly 10,000 acres of strawberries grown annually in Plant City, the Winter Strawberry Capital of the World, it's only appropriate that their harvest is given a proper celebration. Since 1930, the Florida Strawberry Festival has striven to provide visitors with a family-friendly event that has something to offer everyone, including twenty-four headline entertainers, seven livestock shows, a midway of ninety-plus attractions, hundreds of concessionaires, free entertainment acts, competitive exhibits and more—all paying homage to the strawberry. In just eleven days, over 500,000 visitors get a taste of Plant City's hometown pride and love for its agricultural roots.

303 North Lemon Street • Plant City, FL 33563
813.752.9194 • www.flstrawberryfestival.com
Facebook: FLStrawberryFestival

Strawberry Cake

Cake:

3 cups all-purpose flour
2 cups sugar
1½ tablespoons baking powder
½ teaspoon salt
¾ cup vegetable oil
1 cup chopped fresh strawberries
1 teaspoon vanilla extract
4 large eggs, beaten
Red food coloring, optional

Preheat oven to 350°. Butter 2 (9-inch) round cake pans. In a large bowl, mix together all ingredients; evenly divide between prepared pans. Bake 25 to 30 minutes. Top of cake should be springy to touch and a toothpick inserted in center should come out clean.

Frosting:

8 to 10 fresh strawberries plus more for decorating
1 teaspoon sugar
1 (16-ounce) box powdered sugar
1 (8-ounce) package cream cheese, softened
1 teaspoon lemon juice
Red food coloring, optional

In a blender, purée strawberries with white sugar. Taste and add additional sugar if needed. You should have ¼ cup purée. Combine with remaining ingredients using an electric mixer. (If consistency is too thick, add additional strawberry purée.) Frost between layers and outside of cake. Use whole or sliced strawberries to decorate top of cake.

Lee Barker, Florida Strawberry Festival

Strawberry Blush Cake

Cake:

1 box yellow cake mix
3 tablespoons flour
1 (3-ounce) box strawberry Jell-O
1 cup vegetable oil
¾ cup frozen strawberries, thawed
¼ cup milk
4 eggs, separated

In a bowl, mix together cake mix, flour, Jell-O, oil, strawberries, milk and egg yolks. Beat egg whites until stiff; gently fold into cake mixture. Bake in 2 (9-inch) pans at 325° for 35 minutes; remove from pans and cool.

Strawberry Blush Frosting:

1 (16-ounce) box powdered sugar
¼ cup butter, softened
¾ cup frozen strawberries, thawed (divided)
Chopped pecans, optional

In a bowl, combine powdered sugar, butter and ½ cup strawberries; mix well. If too stiff, add remaining ¼ cup strawberries. Spread between cake layers and over cake. Top with pecans, if desired.

Gladys McRae, Bradford County Strawberry Festival

Bradford County Strawberry Festival

Starke • 2nd Weekend in April

The Bradford County Strawberry Festival is a family-friendly event even the four-legged family members are allowed to attend, as long as they are on a leash. More than 200 vendors participated in 2016, with over 15,000 guests attending. We have special music both days. Saturday, we are open from 9 am to 7 pm and Sunday from 9 am to 5 pm. We have kids' rides, free small train rides, and much more. This is a free event with no entry or parking fees. Come out and enjoy the sweetest strawberries this side of Heaven.

100 East Call Street • Starke, FL 32091
904.964.5278 • www.bradfordcountystrawberryfestival.com
Facebook: bradfordcountystrawberryfestival

Poor Man's Cake

My great grandmother, Grandma Klein, called this her Poor Man's Cake, which I never understood because sugar, eggs, and flour can get expensive. It is, however, a great recipe that's simple to make.

- ¾ cup shortening
- 1¾ cups sugar
- 1 egg, beaten
- 4 cups flour
- ½ teaspoon baking soda
- 1 teaspoon ground cloves
- 1 teaspoon allspice

Using an electric mixer, cream shortening and sugar. Add egg and 1 cup water; mix well. In a separate bowl, combine flour, baking soda, cloves and allspice. Add dry ingredients to mixer and beat well. Pour batter into greased and floured Bundt or tube pan; bake at 325° for 1 hour or until a toothpick inserted in the center comes out clean.

Stephanie Owler Loudermilk, Titusville
in honor of her Grandma Klein

Mama's Hickory Nut Cake

My family has been in Florida since the early 1900s and has passed recipes from generation to generation. One of the favorites is Mama's Hickory Nut Cake. It's a family tradition to serve this cake whenever there is a family gathering. I hope you enjoy it.

- 1 cup butter, softened
- 1 cup sugar
- 3½ cups flour, sifted
- 1 teaspoon baking powder
- ½ teaspoon baking soda
- 1 cup buttermilk
- ½ teaspoon salt
- 1 teaspoon vanilla extract
- 2 cups chopped pecans
- 7 egg whites, beaten

Cream butter and sugar. In a separate bowl, combine flour with baking powder and baking soda. Add to creamed mixture; mix well. Add remaining ingredients in order given, mixing well and ending by folding in egg whites. Bake in a prepared tube pan in a preheated 325° oven 90 minutes.

Jamie Martin, Newberry
Pampered Chef

Caramel Pound Cake

2 sticks margarine, softened
½ cup butter-flavored shortening
1 (16-ounce) box light brown sugar
1 cup sugar
5 eggs
3 cups all-purpose flour
½ teaspoon baking powder
1 cup milk
1 teaspoon vanilla extract

Preheat oven to 350°. Cream butter, shortening and both sugars. Add eggs 1 a time, beating well after each. Mix flour and baking powder in a separate bowl. Alternate adding a little flour and a little milk beating well after each addition. Add vanilla and continue beating about 2 more minutes. Pour into a greased and floured tube pan. Bake 1 hour and 15 minutes.

Caramel Glaze:

1 cup packed light brown sugar
½ cup evaporated milk
1 teaspoon vanilla extract
1 cup sugar
1 stick butter
1 cup chopped pecans, optional

Combine all glaze ingredients (except nuts) in a medium saucepan. Bring to a full rolling boil and boil 2 minutes. Add nuts (if desired) and pour over cake. Let cool before serving.

Sour Cream Pound Cake

This recipe is from my great Aunt, Mrs. McDaniel. It's popular with our family and friends and was even published in a cookbook and newspaper in the 1970s.

3 cups sifted all-purpose flour
½ teaspoon baking soda
2 sticks margarine, softened
3 cups sugar
6 eggs
1 cup sour cream
1 teaspoon lemon extract
1 teaspoon vanilla extract

Sift flour with baking soda; set aside. Cream margarine; slowly add sugar, beating well. Add eggs, 1 at a time, beating after each addition. Stir in sour cream. Add flour mixture, ½ cup at a time, beating constantly. Add lemon and vanilla extracts. Pour batter into a greased 10-inch tube pan. Bake at 350° for 1½ hours or until cake is done. Cool cake in pan 5 minutes before removing.

Jamie Martin, Newberry
Pampered Chef

Salted Caramel Butter Cake

Absolutely delicious. This cake is super moist and very rich. I like it so much I have it for breakfast with my coffee and as a dessert with a little vanilla ice cream.

Cake:

3 cups all-purpose flour
2 cups sugar
1 teaspoon salt
½ teaspoon cream of tartar
1 teaspoon baking powder
½ teaspoon baking soda
1 cup caramel coffee creamer
1 cup unsalted butter, room temperature
2 teaspoons vanilla extract
4 large eggs, room temperature

Preheat oven to 325°. Grease and flour a 10-inch Bundt pan. In a large bowl, whisk together flour, sugar, salt, cream of tartar, baking powder and baking soda. With a hand blender (or stand mixer) blend in the coffee creamer, butter, vanilla and eggs. Beat 3 minutes on medium speed. Pour batter into prepared pan and bake 50 to 55 minutes or until wooden toothpick inserted into center comes out clean. Prick holes in the cake while it is still warm. (I use the handle of a wooden spoon.) Slowly pour the Butter Sauce over cake making sure it gets in all the holes. Cool completely before removing from pan. Run knife along edges first to help cake come out cleaner.

Butter Sauce:

¾ cup sugar
⅓ cup butter
3 tablespoons caramel coffee creamer
2 teaspoon vanilla extract

In a saucepan combine sugar, butter and creamer. Cook over medium heat until melted (do not let mixture boil). Remove from heat and stir in vanilla.

Laurie Paddack Wilkes, Fort Myers

Chocolate Fudge Cake

A slice of this cake and a glass milk is heaven.

1 box yellow cake mix plus ingredients to prepare
1 cup margarine
3 cups sugar
⅔ cup milk
1 (12-ounce) bag semisweet chocolate chips

Prepare cake in 3 (8-inch) layers according to directions on box. Cool; split each layer to create 6 layers. In a heavy saucepan, bring margarine, sugar, and milk to full rolling boil. Boil 2 minutes stirring constantly. Remove from heat and add chocolate chips; stir briskly until chocolate is melted. Continue to beat with spoon until icing is thick and has lost most of its shine. Place 1 cake layer on a serving plate and pour icing over top; repeat with 4 more layers. Place last layer on top and pour remaining icing over top allowing it to drip over sides. Cool before slicing.

Chocolate Chocolate Cream Cake

This cake is ultra-rich and well worth the effort.

- 8 (1-ounce) squares unsweetened chocolate
- 2¼ cups sifted all-purpose flour
- 2 teaspoons baking soda
- ½ teaspoon salt
- ½ cup margarine, softened
- 2¼ cups packed light brown sugar
- 3 eggs
- 2½ teaspoons vanilla extract, divided
- 1 cup sour cream
- 1 cup boiling water
- ⅔ cup powdered sugar
- 1 pint heavy cream
- ½ cup unsweetened cocoa powder

Melt chocolate in a double boiler (or in a small glass bowl over hot water or in the microwave); cool. Preheat oven to 350°. Sift together flour, baking soda and salt; set aside. Beat margarine, light brown sugar and eggs at high speed until light and fluffy. Beat in 1½ teaspoons vanilla and cooled chocolate. Stir in dry ingredients and sour cream a little at a time, mixing on low speed until smooth. Stir in boiling water to make a thin batter. Pour into 2 greased 9-inch cake pans. Bake 35 minutes or until center springs back when lightly pressed with fingertips. Split each layer in half horizontally to make 4 layers. Whip powdered sugar, cream, cocoa and remaining 1 teaspoon vanilla until stiff. Spread between layers and over cake. Cool before serving.

Milky Way Cake

This is possibly the best candy-bar cake ever. Wait until you see how the grocery checker looks at you when buying eleven Milky Way bars. Buy a diet Coke, too, just for fun.

11 Milky Way bars, divided
3 sticks butter, softened and divided
2 cups sugar
4 eggs
2½ cups all-purpose flour

1 cup buttermilk
½ teaspoon baking powder
3 teaspoons vanilla extract, divided
2 cups powdered sugar

Melt 8 Milky Way bars with 1 stick butter in a double boiler until smooth. While melting, cream sugar and 1 stick butter. Add eggs, 1 at a time, beating until smooth. And flour, buttermilk and baking powder. Add Milky Way mixture and 2 teaspoons vanilla; mix well. Bake in a greased and floured Bundt or tube pan 40 minutes to 1 hour at 325°. Check for doneness with a toothpick. Cool completely before icing. Melt remaining 3 candy bars and remaining stick of butter until smooth; stir in remaining 1 teaspoon vanilla. Add 1 cup powdered sugar and beat. Continue adding powdered sugar until desired thickness for icing. Spread over top and sides of cake.

Cindy Walker, Lakeland

Lake Hollingsworth, Lakeland

Black-Bottom Cupcakes

1 box chocolate cake mix plus ingredients to prepare
⅓ cup sugar
1 (8-ounce) package cream cheese, softened
1 egg
Dash salt
1 (6-ounce) package semisweet chocolate chips (1 cup)

Prepare cake mix according to package directions. Place paper baking cups in muffin pan; fill each two-thirds full. Cream sugar and cream cheese; add egg and salt. Stir in chocolate pieces. Drop 1 rounded teaspoon of cream cheese mixture onto each cupcake. Bake per package directions. Delicious cream cheese filling makes it unnecessary to frost cupcakes.

Chocolate Lover's Cheesecake

1½ cups (about 18) finely crushed Oreos
3 tablespoons margarine, melted
3 (8-ounce) packages cream cheese, softened
1 (14-ounce) can sweetened condensed milk
3 (1-ounce) squares semisweet chocolate
2 tablespoons instant coffee
3 eggs
2 tablespoons vanilla extract
1 cup mini chocolate chips, divided
Whipped cream

Preheat oven to 300°. Combine cookie crumbs and margarine; press into bottom of a 9-inch springform pan. In a large mixing bowl, beat cream cheese until fluffy. Gradually beat in milk until smooth. Soften chocolate squares in microwave; dissolve instant coffee in 1 tablespoon warm water. Add softened chocolate, coffee, eggs and vanilla to cream cheese mixture; mix well. Stir in ¾ cup chocolate chips. Pour mixture into pan. Bake 1 hour or until center is set. Cool and chill in refrigerator. Garnish with whipped cream and remaining ¼ cup chocolate chips. For a more impressive presentation, garnish with whipped cream, white chocolate curls, and strawberries dipped in white chocolate.

Toffee Cheesecake Bars

⅔ cup butter, softened
¾ cup packed brown sugar
2 cups flour
½ cup chopped pecans
1 (16-ounce) package cream cheese, softened
¾ cup sugar
2 large eggs
1 tablespoon lemon juice
2 teaspoons vanilla extract
1 (7-ounce) Heath Bar, crushed

Preheat oven to 350°. Using an electric mixer, beat butter at medium speed until light. Add brown sugar gradually, beating until fluffy. Add flour and mix well. Stir in pecans. Set aside 1 cup mixture. Press remaining mixture over bottom of a greased 9x13-inch baking pan. Bake 14 to 15 minutes or until light brown. Beat cream cheese at medium speed until smooth. Add sugar gradually, beating until light and fluffy. Beat in eggs 1 at a time. Stir in lemon juice and vanilla. Pour over hot crust. Sprinkle reserved crumb mixture over batter. Bake 25 minutes or until nearly set. (Cheescake will firm up when chilled.) Sprinkle candy over hot cheesecake. Cook on a wire rack. Chill, covered, 8 hours. Cut into bars to serve.

Sweet Corn Cheesecakes

This was one of my favorite dishes from the Mexican Pavilion at Epcot. I loved it and had a bite when I could while working at Disney World. This version can be made into a full-sized cheesecake or mini individual servings.

Crust:

1 pound graham crackers, crushed
1 stick unsalted butter

Preheat oven to 335°. Spray an 8-inch springform pan with cooking spray. Melt butter. Mix with the graham crackers and press into the bottom of the pan, covering the bottom and sides. Set aside. If you are making mini cheesecakes, then press into small, mini muffin pans and set aside.

Cheesecake Filling:

1 (8-ounce) package of cream cheese, softened
6 tablespoons butter, softened
1 (14-ounce) can sweetened condensed milk
3 eggs
1 (12-ounce) can evaporated milk
2 (12-ounce) cans sweet corn, drained

In the bowl of stand mixer fitted with a paddle attachment, beat cream cheese and butter until fully combined and soft. Add sweetened condensed milk and mix until fully blended. Scrape down the sides to make sure everything is well combined. Add eggs one at a time, scraping down sides. Add in evaporated milk a little at a time, scraping the bowl down often. Every time you add something, be sure to scrape down the sides. Add corn to the mixture. Scrape sides and blend all ingredients together. Pour into the springform pan or spoon into the mini portions. Bake 45 minutes to 1 hour or until just set for a whole cheese cake. Mini versions should be checked after about 30 minutes. Rotate as needed. Remove from oven and cool until cheesecake reaches room temperature. Chill for at least 2 hours before serving.

Tasha Koetsch, Orlando
Wanderlust Boudoir by TK Photographies

White Chocolate Key Lime Cheesecake

Crust:

2 tablespoons butter, melted
2 tablespoons sugar
1½ cups graham cracker crumbs

Combine and pat into bottom of 10-inch springform pan.

Filling:

2 pounds cream cheese, softened
½ pint heavy cream
1 cup sour cream
4 eggs, beaten
2 cups sugar
1 tablespoon butter, melted
4 tablespoons flour
1 tablespoon cornstarch
9 ounces white chocolate, melted
Juice from 4 Key limes
2 tablespoons vanilla extract

Beat cream cheese until smooth; add remaining ingredients. Pour onto Crust. Bake at 350° for 1 hour; turn oven off and leave for half an hour without opening door. Chill 12 hours before removing from pan.

Cookies & Candies

Sarasota Skyline

Chocolate Gooey Butter Cookies

1 (8-ounce) package cream cheese, softened
1 stick butter, softened
1 egg
1 teaspoon vanilla extract
1 box moist chocolate cake mix
Powdered sugar for coating

Preheat oven to 350°. Using an electric mixer, beat cream cheese and butter until smooth. Add egg; mix well. Add vanilla and cake mix; beat well. Cover and chill 2 hours. Roll chilled dough into tablespoon-size balls; roll in powdered sugar to coat. Place 2 inches apart on an ungreased cookie sheet. Bake 12 minutes. Cookies will remain soft and gooey. Cool completely and sprinkle with additional powdered sugar, if desired.

Chocolate Pinwheel Cookies

½ cup shortening, softened
1 cup sugar
½ cup peanut butter
1 egg
2 tablespoons milk
1¼ cups flour
½ teaspoon salt
½ teaspoon baking soda
2 (8-ounce) packages chocolate chips

Mix shortening, sugar and peanut butter until creamy. Add egg and milk; mix well. In a separate bowl, sift together flour, salt and baking soda. Combine both mixtures into a soft dough. Roll out on floured wax paper to ¼ inch thick. Melt chocolate chips and spread over dough. Roll up and refrigerate 1 hour or longer. When ready to bake, slice cookies ¼ inch thick. Place on greased cookie sheet and bake at 350° for 10 minutes or until light brown. Cool 3 minutes on cookie sheet them remove to serving dish.

Your Favorite Chocolate Cookies

If these aren't your favorite chocolate cookies, they soon will be.

- 2½ sticks unsalted butter, softened
- 2 cups sugar plus more for topping
- 2 large eggs
- 1 tablespoon vanilla extract
- ¾ cup Dutch process cocoa powder
- 2 cups all-purpose flour
- 1 teaspoon baking soda
- ½ teaspoon salt

In a large bowl, cream butter and sugar with a hand mixer. Add eggs and vanilla; mix until combined. In a separate bowl, mix cocoa powder, flour, baking soda and salt. Slowly add dry ingredients to creamed mixture; mix well. Roll dough into 2 logs (about 2 inches wide and 12 inches long). Wrap in wax paper and place in the refrigerator 2 hours. Preheat oven to 350°. Once thoroughly chilled, slice dough into ½-inch-thick rounds and cover with sugar. Place on a parchment-lined cookie sheet and bake 10 minutes. Remove to a wire rack to cool.

Grandma Hall's No-Bakes

This is my Grandma Hall's family favorite 'No-Bakes' recipe. We all knew when she said 'No-Bakes,' she was whipping up a batch of her peanut butter no-bake cookies. My grandfather Earl B. Hall was a member of the 95th infantry Iron Men of Metz in the U.S. Army and loves these cookies almost as much as my grandmother loved making them for him.

2 cups sugar
½ cup milk
¼ stick margarine
¼ cup cocoa powder
3 cups quick oats
½ cup peanut butter, smooth or crunchy
1 teaspoon vanilla extract
Dash salt

Bring sugar, milk, margarine and cocoa to a boil in a saucepan over medium heat, stirring occasionally. Boil 1 minute; remove from heat. Add oats, peanut butter, vanilla and salt; stir to combine, coating oats completely. Drop by the spoonful onto wax paper and cool.

Stephanie Owler Loudermilk, Titusville
in honor of her grandparents Bonita and Earl Hall

Ramen Noodle–Chocolate Butterscotch Cookies

2 (3-ounce) packages Ramen noodles, crushed
2 cups chocolate chips
⅔ cup butterscotch chips
2 tablespoons oil

Crush uncooked noodles into small pieces (toss seasoning packets). In a microwave-safe bowl, combine chocolate chips, butterscotch chips and oil. Microwave 15 seconds, remove and stir. Repeat with 15 then 10 second cook times until fully melted and smooth. Add broken noodles and stir until fully coated. Drop by the spoonful onto a cookie sheet covered with wax paper. Chill, uncovered, until set.

Jared Poulson, Orlando

Chocolate Toffee Bars

1¾ cups crushed chocolate teddy bear graham cracker cookies
1 stick butter, melted
1 (6-ounce) package milk chocolate chips
1 (6-ounce) package almond brickle chips
1 (6-ounce) package white chocolate chips
1 cup chopped walnuts
1 cup chopped pecans
1 (14-ounce) can sweetened condensed milk

Line a 9x13-inch pan with heavy-duty aluminum foil. Spread crushed cookies in pan and pour melted butter over them. Bake at 325° for 5 minutes. Remove from oven. Layer all chips and nuts over cookie layer, pressing into bottom layer. Pour sweetened condensed milk over all. Bake 30 minutes. Cool completely. Cut into squares, removing foil.

White Chocolate-Cherry Chunk Cookies

½ cup butter, softened
1 cup sugar
1 cup packed brown sugar
2 large eggs
1 teaspoon vanilla extract
3 cups all-purpose flour

1 teaspoon baking soda
½ teaspoon salt
2 tablespoons milk
1 cup chopped macadamia nuts
½ cup candied cherries
1½ cups white chocolate chunks

Preheat oven to 375°. With an electric mixer, cream butter and sugars together until light and fluffy. Add eggs and vanilla; set aside. Sift together flour, soda and salt. Stir into creamed mixture along with milk. In another bowl, combine nuts, cherries and white chocolate; stir into dough just enough to blend. Drop by heaping tablespoons 2 inches apart onto a greased cookie sheet. Bake 11 to 13 minutes. Cool on wire rack. Makes about 4 dozen cookies.

Butter Pecan Cookies

Captain Jordan Todd of Saltwater Obsessions guide service in Port St. Joe is a third-generation fisherman who grew up on the Gulf Coast. One of his favorite memories is the smell of fresh-baked Pecan Cookies. He still loves them to this day and decided to pass along a recipe. "I think my original recipe came from a bag of pecans or something, so I can't take full credit. But these are one of my favorite cookies! A dash of brown sugar adds a big of extra flavor."

> 1 stick unsalted butter, room temperature
> ⅓ cup sugar
> 1 teaspoon packed brown sugar
> 1 teaspoon vanilla extract
> ⅛ teaspoon salt
> 1 cup all-purpose flour
> ¾ cup pecans, chopped

Combine everything in a bowl except pecans. Mix with an electric mixer until you get the dough consistency and then fold in pecans. Pinch pieces of the dough off and roll into balls. Makes 12 to 14 balls. Place on a cookie sheet with space between them and flatten gently with the bottom of a glass. Bake at 350° about 10 minutes. Rotate cookie sheet and bake an additional 5 minutes. Cool cookies on a wire rack.

Captain Jordan Todd, Port St. Joe
Saltwater Obsessions Guide Service

Chewy Pecan Supreme Cookies

> ½ cup shortening
> 1½ cups packed brown sugar
> 2 eggs
> 1 teaspoon vanilla extract
> 1½ cups self-rising flour
> 1 cup crushed cornflakes
> 1½ cups chopped pecans

Cream shortening, sugar, eggs and vanilla. Add flour; mix well. Add cornflakes and pecans; mix well. Drop by teaspoonful on a cookie sheet treated with nonstick spray. Bake at 350° for 10 minutes. Cool before serving.

Pecan Tassies

Crust:
1¾ cups all-purpose flour
6 tablespoons sugar
1¾ sticks cold butter
1 large egg yolk
1 tablespoon vanilla extract

Combine flour and sugar in a food processor. Add butter and pulse until mixture resembles coarse meal. Add egg yolk and vanilla; blend just until moist clumps form. Divide dough into 10 pieces. Press 1 piece onto bottom and up sides of each of 10 tartlet pans with removable bottom (or well-greased mini muffin tins). Freeze 15 minutes.

Filling:
2 large eggs
½ cup packed brown sugar
¼ cup light corn syrup
¼ cup molasses
4 tablespoons butter, melted
1 tablespoon vanilla extract
1½ cups coarsely chopped pecans

Position rack in bottom third of oven and preheat to 350°. Whisk together all ingredients, except pecans, in a large bowl. Fold in chopped pecans. Divide filling among prepared crusts. Bake until filling is firm and crusts are golden, about 30 minutes. Cool slightly. Serve warm or at room temperature.

Lemon-Cream Cheese Cookies

1 lemon
2 sticks butter, softened
½ (8-ounce) package cream cheese, softened
1 cup sugar
1 egg, beaten
2½ cups flour
1 teaspoon baking powder

Zest lemon for 2½ teaspoons; set aside. Juice lemon for 4 tablespoons juice; set aside. Using an electric mixer, blend butter and cream cheese. Add sugar; cream thoroughly. Add egg, 1 tablespoon lemon juice and 1 teaspoon zest (reserve remaining juice and zest for glaze); blend well. In a separate bowl, mix flour and baking powder. Add to cream cheese mixture; mix well. Wrap dough in plastic wrap and chill at least 30 minutes. Preheat oven to 375°. Using about 1½ tablespoons dough, roll into balls and place on an ungreased cookie sheet. Bake 14 to 16 minutes. Cool 10 minutes on cookie sheet then remove to wire rack to completely cool.

Lemon Glaze:

2 cups powdered sugar
1 teaspoon vanilla extract

Whisk powdered sugar and vanilla with reserved 3 tablespoons lemon juice and 1½ teaspoons zest. If glaze seems too thick, add 1 teaspoon water at a time until it reaches a glaze consistency. Drizzle over cooled cookies and let sit until glaze sets.

Lemon Finger Cookies

The best summer cookie ever requires no baking and pairs perfectly with a cold glass of lemonade.

1 (11-ounce) box vanilla wafer cookies, crushed
3 cups flaked coconut
2 sticks butter, melted
1 (12-ounce) can sweetened condensed milk
1 lemon, juiced
2 cups powdered sugar

In a bowl, combine wafer crumbs, coconut and butter; mix well. Add condensed milk and mix thoroughly. Press into bottom of a 9x9-inch baking pan. Combine lemon juice and powdered sugar in a bowl; mix until smooth. Pour over crumb mixture. Chill 1 hour. Cut into squares.

Lemon Crumb Squares

1 (14-ounce) can sweetened condensed milk
1 teaspoon grated lemon rind
½ cup lemon juice
1½ cups flour
½ teaspoon salt
1 teaspoon baking powder
1 cup uncooked quick oats
⅔ cup butter, softened
1 cup packed dark brown sugar

Preheat oven to 350°. Blend milk, lemon rind and juice for filling; set aside. Sift flour, salt and baking powder into a bowl; add oats. Using an electric mixer, cream butter and sugar. Add flour mixture and beat until crumbly. Spread half in a buttered 9x9-inch pan and pat down. Spread filling over top. Crumble remaining oat mixture on top. Bake 25 minutes. Cool in pan 15 minutes. Cut into squares. Chill in pan until firm.

Raspberry Star Cookies

2 cups all-purpose flour
2 tablespoons sugar
½ teaspoon salt
¾ cup (1½ sticks) unsalted butter, chilled and chopped
1 (12-ounce) jar raspberry preserves

Mix flour, sugar and salt in a food processor. Add butter and pulse until mixture resembles coarse meal. Add 6 to 8 tablespoons ice water gradually, mixing just until mixture is moist enough to be pressed together. Turn out onto a lightly floured surface and press into a ball. Set aside a quarter of the dough. Roll remaining large portion into a ¼-inch-thick rectangle and place on a cookie sheet. Freeze 30 minutes. Prick pastry all over with a fork. Bake at 400° for 10 minutes. Cool on a wire rack. Spread with preserves. Roll remaining dough ⅛ inch thick. Cut into star shapes using a cookie cutter. Place stars over preserves with points touching. Bake at 350 ° for 15 to 20 minutes or until light brown. Cool on a wire rack and cut into squares (1 star per cookie.)

Snickerdoodle Cookies

I believe in family, learning more and improving your life. And I think that sometimes you just can't beat a good snickerdoodle! I thought I would pass this recipe along for everyone to learn. My suggestion is to use butter, not margarine or low-fat butter. Hope you enjoy.

—Ryan Knuppel

2 sticks butter, room temperature
1 cup sugar, divided
½ cup packed brown sugar
1 large egg
1 tablespoon vanilla extract

1 teaspoon baking soda
1 teaspoon cream of tartar
½ teaspoon salt
4 teaspoons ground cinnamon, divided
2¾ cup flour

In a stand mixer, mix butter, ¾ cup sugar and brown sugar together; add egg, vanilla, baking soda, cream of tartar, salt and 1 teaspoon cinnamon. Mix well before adding in flour. Mix completely while being sure to scrape the sides of bowl. Combine remaining sugar and remaining cinnamon in a small bowl or dish and set aside. Separate dough into 20 portions and roll into balls. Roll each ball in the sugar-cinnamon mixture and place on a nonstick cookie sheet or one lined with parchment paper. Bake in a preheated 325° oven for 10 to 12 minutes. Rotate pan halfway through. Allow to cool before serving.

Ryan Knuppel, Orlando
www.rewrittenlife.com

Key Lime Cookies

1 to 2 fresh Key limes
1 stick butter, softened
1½ cups powdered sugar
1 egg
1 cup flour
1 teaspoon baking powder
¼ teaspoon salt
2 cups crushed cornflakes

Preheat oven to 350°. Zest limes for 2 teaspoons zest; squeeze for 1 tablespoon juice. Cream butter and sugar in a mixing bowl until light and fluffy. Stir in egg, Key lime juice and zest. Add flour, baking powder and salt; mix well. Place crushed cornflakes in a shallow bowl. Drop dough by teaspoonfuls into cornflakes and turn to coat. Place on ungreased cookie sheets. Bake 16 minutes. Remove to a wire rack to cool. Makes 2 dozen cookies.

Key Lime Fudge

3 to 4 fresh Key limes
3 cups (18 ounces) white chocolate chips
1 (14-ounce) can sweetened condensed milk
1 cup toasted, chopped macadamia nuts

Zest limes for 2 teaspoons zest; squeeze for 2 tablespoons juice. Line an 8x8-inch (or 9x9-inch) dish with foil, allowing a 4- to 5-inch overhang. Coat foil with butter. Combine white chocolate chips and condensed milk in heavy saucepan. Cook, stirring frequently, over low heat just until chocolate melts and mixture is smooth. Remove from heat. Stir in lime juice and lime zest. Add macadamia nuts and mix well. Spread in prepared dish and chill, covered, 2 hours or until firm. Lift fudge out of dish using edges of foil. Cut into squares and store in an airtight container at room temperature up to 1 week or freeze up to 2 months.

Coconut Macaroons

3 egg whites
1 cup sugar
3 cups shredded coconut
2 tablespoons cornstarch
1 tablespoon vanilla extract

Beat egg whites until stiff but not dry. Gradually beat sugar into egg whites. In a separate bowl, combine coconut and cornstarch tossing to mix well. Fold into egg whites. Cook in double boiler over hot water, stirring often, 15 minutes. Add vanilla; stir just until combined. Drop by teaspoonfuls, 1 inch apart, onto greased cookie sheet. Bake at 300° for 20 to 25 minutes or until lightly browned. Makes 2½ dozen.

Easy Coconut Dreams

2 sticks butter, softened
½ cup sugar
2 cups flour
1 (4-ounce) can flaked coconut

Cream butter and sugar in a mixing bowl until light and fluffy. Beat in flour and coconut. Shape into 2 logs (1½ inches in diameter). Chill, covered, until firm. Cut logs into ¼-inch-thick slices. Place slices on a nonstick cookie sheet. Bake at 300° for 25 minutes or until coconut is browned. Cool on wire rack. Store in an airtight container. Makes 5 dozen.

Dot's Cream Cheese Gems

1 stick butter, softened
4 ounces cream cheese, softened
1 cup sugar
1 cup flour
½ teaspoon vanilla extract

Cream butter and cream cheese. Add sugar, flour and vanilla. Drop by spoonful onto ungreased cookie sheet. Bake at 350° for 8 to 10 minutes, until slightly colored on bottom.

Stephanie Owler Loudermilk, Titusville

Homemade Tootsie Rolls

Super cute and fun to make.

1 (12-ounce) package semisweet chocolate chips
½ cup light corn syrup
1 teaspoon vanilla extract
½ teaspoon orange extract

Line a cookie sheet (with sides) with wax paper; set aside. Heat chocolate in microwave, 5 to 10 seconds at a time, until melted and smooth. Add ¾ teaspoon warm water, corn syrup, vanilla extract and orange extract. Scrape mixture onto cookie sheet and spread into a 1-inch-thick flat layer. (It is okay for it to not reach sides of pan.) Cover with plastic wrap and rest overnight at room temperature. The next day, remove to a chopping board and cut into ½-inch-wide strips. Roll strips (in your hands or on work surface) to form a log. Cut into serving-size sections and set aside 10 minutes to harden. Wrap in wax paper and serve.

Clewiston • 3rd Saturday in March

The Clewiston Sugar Festival is based on the original end of end-of-harvest celebration that was held by the United States Sugar Corporation, dating back to the 1930s, at the end of each sugarcane harvest season. Over the years, the Sugar Festival has evolved into an exciting multiday event where folks can reunite with family, friends, and neighbors at the end of another busy season. People come from the Glades and from across the state to gather for a day of good times, great live entertainment, cane-grinding, a car show, a kids' park, and a variety of food booths sponsored by local civic, school, and church organizations that offer the best of local cuisine. We raise cane!

Civic Park • Highway 27 • Clewiston, FL 33440
863.983.7979 • www.clewistonsugarfestival.com
Facebook: SugarFestival

Jane's Fancy Bourbon Balls

My mother, Jane Hernandez, shared one of her favorite holiday recipes with me only when I was old enough because it contains bourbon. I always giggle when I make this recipe because of the way she wrote the recipe down—"BOOZE" instead of bourbon.

- 1 cup chocolate chips
- 3 tablespoons white Karo syrup
- ½ cup bourbon (or brandy)
- 2½ cups crushed vanilla wafers
- 1½ cups powdered sugar
- 1 cup chopped nuts

These directions are directly from my mother Jane so enjoy the instructions in her voice. "Melt chocolate over hot water and add Karo syrup and booze. Combine vanilla wafer crumbs, powdered sugar and nuts. Add chocolate mixture and stir. Let stand 30 minutes. Shape into 1-inch balls and roll in powdered sugar. Let ripen in covered container at least 3 days. I usually spread a small cloth soaked in the booze I used over the top and re-soak it each day. If you do this you may have to reroll in sugar after 3 or 4 days. This treatment makes them have a real bite. Without it your cookie is much milder. Makes 4 dozen."

Lisa Barnes, Palm Beach

Taste of Oviedo's Citrus & Celery Cook-Off

Oviedo • 2nd Weekend in March

The Taste of Oviedo Citrus & Celery Cook-Off spotlights nonstop fun with free admission for the whole family. Come enjoy delicious dishes from the best local Oviedo restaurants and eateries while the kids enjoy rides and activities in Kids Taste area. Test your culinary skills by competing in the Citrus & Celery Cook-Off or just sit back and enjoy live music all day.

Oviedo Mall • 1700 Oviedo Mall Boulevard • Oviedo, FL 32765
407.278.4871 • www.tasteofoviedo.org
Facebook: TasteOfOviedo

Chocolate Pretzel Bark with Orange Essence

1 (8-ounce) bag tiny pretzel twists
1 cup butter
1 cup packed brown sugar
¾ cup orange marmalade (low-sugar version is best)
1 orange, zested
2 cups semisweet chocolate chips
Coarse ground sea salt, optional

Preheat oven to 350°. Line 2 jelly-roll pans with parchment paper or aluminum foil. Cover with pretzels laying them side by side. In a medium saucepan over medium heat, melt butter; add sugar, whisking continuously to keep from scorching. Add marmalade and cook, stirring, 10 to 15 minutes. Mixture should turn a darker caramel color and thicken. Stir in orange zest; remove from heat. Drizzle evenly over both trays of pretzels. (Not every surface of the pretzels will be covered.) Place the trays in oven 4 to 5 minutes. Remove pans from oven; sprinkle chocolate evenly over top of pretzels. Return to oven 1 minute. Using a spatula, spread melted chocolate evenly. Sprinkle with sea salt, if desired. Cool to room temperature; freeze 1 to 2 hours. Remove from freezer; peel off parchment or foil. Break bark into serving-size pieces; store in lidded container. Bark tastes best when kept in the fridge or freezer.

Taste of Oviedo's Citrus & Celery Cook-Off
Barbara Cain, Grand Prize winner 2016

Panhandle Buckeye Candy

My wife, Allyson, grew up in Louisiana but lived along the panhandle at West Bay, Florida while working at restaurants during the summer. One of her favorite foods from that time had nothing to do with seafood but with a peanut butter candy that's now one of our family favorites. Allyson makes several batches up every year during Christmas and the holidays. We have some at home while we bag the remaining for all of our family members and friends. "I love making these during the holidays and sharing with family and friends at Christmas. I started making them while I was living and working on the Florida Panhandle in West Bay. A candy company there made them, so I had to learn how to make a batch after I moved. My only suggestion is to use regular peanut butter—not low fat or anything like that. I prefer creamy but have made a few batches with chunky peanut butter."

1½ cups peanut butter, creamy or chunky
1 cup butter, room temperature
½ teaspoon vanilla extract
6 cups powdered sugar
4 cups semisweet chocolate chips
Drop of cooking oil if needed

In a bowl, mix peanut butter with butter, vanilla and powdered sugar. Mix well and fold evenly. Pinch and roll into 1-inch balls and place on a prepared or waxed paper–lined cookie sheet. Press a toothpick into each of the balls, about halfway through. Refrigerate several hours or freeze at least an hour. Melt chocolate chips in a double boiler or in a microwave using the manufacturer's directions, stirring frequently until smooth and creamy. Add a drop or two of oil, if needed, for consistency. When chocolate is ready, dip balls in chocolate while holding the toothpick. Leave a small portion of the top uncovered, so they look like real Ohio State Buckeyes. Gently remove the toothpick and refrigerate until ready to serve.

Allyson Nagem Whitaker, West Bay

Peanut Butter Bonbons

1 cup peanut butter chips
1 cup semisweet chocolate chips
1 tablespoon butter
1 ounce unsweetened chocolate, chopped
½ teaspoon vanilla extract
1½ cups crushed saltine crackers (about 36)
½ cup very finely chopped pecans

Place peanut butter chips, chocolate chips, butter and unsweetened chocolate in saucepan over very low heat. Cook, stirring frequently, until melted. Remove from heat; add vanilla. Stir in cracker crumbs gradually to make a stiff dough. Roll into large marble-size balls. Spread pecans on wax paper; roll each bonbon in pecans to coat. Let stand on wax paper 30 minutes to set. Store in airtight container at room temperature or in freezer. Makes about 50.

Fort Pierce Oyster Festival

Downtown Fort Pierce • April

Fort Pierce Oyster Festival is a two-day festival that celebrates the Fort Pierce Waterfront and all of its bounty with delicious oysters, tasty seafood dishes, landlubber foods, live entertainment, and a bevy of arts and crafts and merchandise vendors. This exciting event features food, music, arts and crafts, and marine education exhibits, not to mention a shipload of oysters. Event patrons will be eating oysters and saving the shells for Oyster Restoration Projects, including the Spoil Islands near the Fort Pierce City Marina.

600 North Indian River Drive • Fort Pierce, FL 34950
772.285.1646 • www.fortpierceoysterfest.com
Facebook: fortpierceoysterfestival

Peanut Butter Chewies

This is my family's version of no-bake cookies. It's really simple to make and perfect for letting kids help. My advice is to let the cookies cool completely before serving. They taste even better the next day.

1 cup white Karo syrup
1 cup sugar
1 cup peanut butter
6 cups Frosted Flakes cereal

Bring Karo syrup and sugar to a boil in a saucepan; remove from heat. Add peanut butter and cereal; stir to coat. Drop by spoonsful onto wax paper. Cool before serving; store in a closed container.

Jamie Martin, Newberry
Pampered Chef

Central Florida Peanut Festival

Williston • 1st Saturday in October

Join more than 9,000 visitors in Williston's Heritage Park to celebrate all things nutty. You are sure to enjoy this thirty-year tradition with peanuts galore and a fun festival including the Little Peanut Royal Family. Crowning of Little Peanut King and Queen and Baby Peanut is one of the highlights of this family festival. Visitors enjoy great food and great fun including arts, crafts, live entertainment, a petting zoo, and more. The family-friendly festival is truly everything peanuts.

Heritage Park • North Main Street • Williston, FL 32696
352.528.5552 • www.willistonfl.com

Virginia's Peanut Butter Candy

½ stick butter, melted
2 cups creamy peanut butter
2 cups crushed graham crackers
¾ to 1 cup powdered sugar
1 (12-ounce) package semisweet chocolate chips

Using the microwave, melt butter in a large bowl; add peanut butter and mix well. Add graham cracker crumbs and mix together. Add powdered sugar and mix with clean hands until well combined and looks like coarse wet sand. Pat evenly into a 9x13-inch pan. Melt chocolate chips in the microwave or double boiler and spread over the top. Let harden, then cut into small bars.

Virginia Ball, Orlando

Island Fruit Bar

1 box moist white cake mix
⅓ cup butter, melted
1 egg, room temperature
1 (12-ounce) bag white chocolate premium chips
1 (10-ounce) bag dried tropical fruit
1 cup flaked coconut
1 cup sliced almonds
1 (14-ounce) can sweetened condensed milk

Preheat oven to 350°. Line a 9x13-inch pan with aluminum foil; spray sides and bottom with nonstick spray. In a large mixing bowl, blend dry cake mix, butter and egg until mixed. Press evenly into bottom of pan. Sprinkle evenly over crust, in this order, white chips, dried fruit, coconut and almonds; press down on topping all around. Pour condensed milk evenly over. Bake 35 to 40 minutes or until golden brown. Remove from oven; cool completely. Remove from pan (don't turn it over); carefully remove foil. Cut in half, then cut each half into 9 pieces. Total 18 bars. Can be wrapped and frozen if it lasts long enough.

Christine M. Cirou, Lorida

Pies & Other Desserts

Florida State Capitol, Tallahassee

Quick Strawberry Pie

1 (3-ounce) package strawberry Jell-O
1 pint frozen or fresh strawberries, crushed
1 (9-inch) baked pie crust
1 (2.6-ounce) envelope Dream Whip plus ingredients to prepare

Dissolve Jell-O in ½ cup boiling water; add strawberries and mix well. Pour into pie crust; cool in refrigerator until set. Top with prepared Dream Whip.

Women of First United Methodist Church, Starke
Bradford County Strawberry Festival

7 Up Strawberry Pie

1 cup sugar
4 tablespoons cornstarch
1 (12-ounce) can 7 Up
1 teaspoon red food coloring
2 pints strawberries, sliced (small berries may be left whole)
1 (9-inch) baked pie crust
1 (8-ounce) container Cool Whip

In a saucepan, cook together, sugar, cornstarch, 7 Up and food coloring until very thick; cool. Stir in strawberries. Pour into pie crust and top with Cool Whip.

Women of First United Methodist Church, Starke
Bradford County Strawberry Festival

Fluffy Strawberry Pie

Growing up, we had great family meals—a favorite was Nana's salmon patties, hushpuppies and my family's famous coleslaw. After dinner, we would enjoy a slice of Fluffy Strawberry Pie. This recipe is very easy and tasty. I hope your family enjoys it as much as our family has.

1 (.3-ounce) package sugar-free strawberry gelatin
¼ cup boiling water
2 (6-ounce) containers strawberry yogurt
1 (8-ounce) container fat-free whipped topping
1 (8-inch) reduced-fat graham cracker pie crust

In a large bowl, dissolve gelatin in boiling water. Whisk in both containers of yogurt until evenly mixed. Fold in whipped topping without over mixing—just enough to blend evenly. Spoon into the crust and spread evenly. Cover and refrigerator at least 2 hours or until set. Slice and serve.

Lisa Barnes, Palm Beach

Deluxe Strawberry Pie

Crust:

3 egg whites
1 cup sugar
23 Ritz crackers, broken in small pieces
1 cup coarsely chopped pecans
1 teaspoon vanilla extract

Beat egg whites until stiff. Gradually add sugar, continuing to beat until stiff peaks are formed. Fold in remaining ingredients. Pour into well-greased pie plate, forming higher around edges to hold filling. Bake at 350° for 30 minutes; cool.

Filling:

1 quart fresh Florida strawberries, sliced
6 tablespoons sugar, divided
1 cup whipping cream

Place sliced strawberries in a small bowl. Stir in 4 tablespoons sugar; set aside a few minutes to marinate. Whip cream with remaining sugar. Drain strawberries; fold in whipped cream. Pour into pie crust; refrigerate at least 2 hours before serving. Serves 6.

Women of First United Methodist Church, Starke
Bradford County Strawberry Festival

Sandy Shoes Seafood Festival

Fort Pierce • 3rd Saturday in March

Sandy Shoes Seafood Festival unfolds along the beautiful Indian River in historic, downtown Fort Pierce. The festival features local Florida seafood, live music, more than 100 arts and crafts vendors, a chowder competition, an iron chef competition, and the popular citrus squeeze-off.

600 North Indian River Drive • Fort Pierce, FL 34950
772.466.3880 • www.sandyshoesseafoodandbrew.com

Strawberry Yogurt Pie

2 cups graham cracker crumbs
⅓ cup melted butter
¼ cup plus ⅓ cup honey, divided
1 (8-ounce) package cream cheese, softened
1 (8-ounce) container strawberry-flavored yogurt
1 (8-ounce) container sour cream
1 teaspoon vanilla extract
½ cup sliced fresh strawberries

Combine cracker crumbs, butter and ¼ cup honey; blend well and press on bottom and sides of a 9-inch pie plate. Freeze at least 30 minutes. Using an electric mixer on medium speed, beat cream cheese until smooth. In a separate bowl, combine yogurt and sour cream; mix well. Add to cream cheese mixture blending until smooth. Stir in vanilla and remaining honey. Pour into crust; freeze until firm. Remove 30 minutes before serving and garnish with strawberries.

Women of First United Methodist Church, Starke
Bradford County Strawberry Festival

Strawberry Chiffon Pie

2 pints strawberries
1 cup sugar, divided
2 (1-ounce) envelopes unflavored gelatin
3 egg whites
1½ cups heavy cream, divided
1 (9-inch) baked pie crust

Wash and hull strawberries. Slice enough to make 3 cups; reserve remainder for garnish. Combine sliced berries and ½ cup sugar in medium-size bowl; let stand 5 minutes. Mash well or press through a sieve into a large bowl. Soften gelatin in ½ cup water in a small saucepan. Heat slowly until gelatin dissolves. Cool slightly, then stir into mashed strawberries. Place bowl in a pan of ice and water to speed setting; chill, in refrigerator, stirring several times, until mixture begins to thicken. While gelatin mixture chills, beat egg whites in a medium-size bowl until foamy white; slowly beat in remaining ½ cup sugar until meringue stands in firm peaks. In a separate bowl, beat 1 cup cream until stiff. Fold meringue, then whipped cream, into strawberry mixture until no streaks of white remain. Pour into cooled pastry shell. Chill several hours, or until firm. Just before serving, beat remaining cream in a small bowl until stiff; spoon onto center of pie. Garnish with remaining strawberries.

Women of First United Methodist Church, Starke
Bradford County Strawberry Festival

Florida Orange Pie

Pie:
9 to 10 medium oranges
1 cup sugar
2 tablespoons cornstarch
½ teaspoon salt
1 tablespoon butter
3 eggs, separated
1 (9-inch) pie crust, baked

Peel and section 1 orange; set aside. Zest oranges to get 3 tablespoons; set aside. Juice oranges to get 2 cups juice. Combine orange juice and sugar in a saucepan over medium heat; boil until sugar dissolves. In a small bowl, whisk together cornstarch and equal parts water; add to orange juice mixture. Add salt and butter; mix. In a separate bowl, beat egg yolks (refrigerate egg whites for meringue); add a little of hot mixture and stir together. Add back to saucepan and cooking, stirring, until thickened. Add orange zest and orange sections; remove from heat. Pour into pie crust; cool.

Meringue Topping:
3 egg whites (reserved from pie recipe)
3 tablespoons ice water
Pinch salt
6 tablespoons sugar

Preheat oven to 300°. Beat egg whites until frothy. Add ice water and then salt; beat. Add sugar, 1 tablespoon at a time, beating continuously. Continue to beat until whites reach stiff peaks. Spread over cooled pie, sealing to edges. Bake 15 to 20 minutes or until brown.

Orange-Pecan Pie

1 medium orange, quartered
1½ cups packed brown sugar
1 cup light corn syrup
3 tablespoons butter
3 eggs, well beaten
1½ cups chopped pecans
1 (9-inch) unbaked pie crust

Preheat oven to 350°. Removed seeds from orange and process in a food processor (peel and pulp). In a saucepan over medium-high heat, combine ground orange, sugar and corn syrup. Bring to a roiling boil. Remove from heat. Cool 5 minutes, stirring occasionally. Add butter and cool another 5 minutes, continuing to stir occasionally. Beat in eggs and pecans mixing well. Pour into pie crust and bake 40 to 45 minutes or until set.

Margaritaville Key Lime Pie

1 (9-inch) graham cracker pie crust
6 eggs, divided
1 (14-ounce) can sweetened condensed milk
½ cup Key lime juice
2 teaspoons cream of tartar
½ cup sugar

Bake pie crust at 350° for 5 minutes. Separate 2 eggs (careful not to get any egg yolk in whites); set whites aside in a bowl in refrigerator (will use for topping). Beat egg yolks with an electric mixer 2 minutes; add condensed milk and beat well. Separate another egg; discard yolk and beat egg white with electric mixer until fluffy. Gently fold into egg yolk mixture. Fold in lime juice. Pour filling into pie crust. Refrigerate 2 to 3 hours before topping with meringue. Separate remaining 3 eggs; discard yolks. Whip whites with 2 reserved egg whites and cream of tartar using an electric mixer until foamy. Continue to whip while slowly adding sugar. Beat until stiff peaks form. Spread over filling sealing to edges. Bake at 425° for 5 minutes or until topping browns slightly.

The Key Lime Festival

Key West • 4th of July Weekend

The Key Lime Festival is America's favorite citrus celebration. In the Florida Keys, locals like to celebrate the things that make the islands unique: citrus, eccentrics, people, and pie. While the celebrations are fun, odd, and unforgettable, visitors will soon discover that the people are, too. From pie-eating contests to culinary classes and pie hops to fireworks, come on down to the birthplace of Key Lime Pie for a little taste, and you will see what we mean. Love & Limes.

305.923.7822 • www.keylimefestival.com
Facebook: KeyLimeFestival

Black-Bottom Walnut Pie

1 (9-inch) unbaked pie crust
6 ounces dark chocolate, melted
1 cup sugar
4 ounces heavy cream
6 ounces sour cream
¼ teaspoon salt
2 tablespoons bourbon
½ teaspoon vanilla extract
2 eggs, beaten
10 ounces walnut pieces (about 2 cups)

Preheat oven to 375°. Prick bottom of pie crust with a fork and bake until lightly brown, about 12 minutes. Reduce oven temperature to 325°. Using pastry brush, coat pie crust with melted chocolate. In a medium saucepan, cook sugar and 2 tablespoons water over medium heat until caramelized. Add cream, stirring constantly; remove from heat. Add sour cream, salt, bourbon and vanilla; mix well. Add eggs, beating quickly to prevent them scrambling. Fold in walnuts and pour into crust. Bake 1 hour.

Chocolate Cheese Pie

Crust:

3 cups flour
1 cup powdered sugar
½ teaspoon baking powder
½ cup shortening
2 eggs
½ teaspoon vanilla extract

Mix flour, sugar and baking powder. Cut in shortening until crumbly. Separate eggs; reserve whites in refrigerator for filling. Beat egg yolks; mix in vanilla and ¼ cup water. Add to flour mixture and mix well by hand. Reserve a quarter of dough for lattice strips. Roll out remaining dough to ¼ inch, and line bottom of a 3-quart oblong baking dish.

Cheese Filling:

6 eggs
3 pounds ricotta cheese
1½ teaspoons lemon extract
1 tablespoon vanilla extract
1 teaspoon orange extract
1 cup sugar
⅛ teaspoon salt

Separate eggs (careful to not allow any yolk in the egg white); reserve 1 yolk for chocolate mixture. Beat egg whites plus the 2 egg whites reserved from crust until fluffy. Add remaining ingredients beating well; set aside.

Chocolate Filling:

4 (1-ounce) squares semisweet chocolate
2 tablespoons sugar

Preheat oven to 350°. Melt chocolate. Blend in sugar and reserved egg yolk. Set aside. Pour half the Cheese Filling into crust. Drop Chocolate Filling randomly over the top. Then top with remaining Cheese Filling. Swirl with a knife to create a marbled effect. Roll reserved dough to ⅛ inch thick. Cut into strips and form a lattice over pie. Bake 1 hour.

Impossible French Apple Pie

6 tart apples, sliced
1¼ teaspoons ground cinnamon
¼ teaspoon ground nutmeg
1 cup sugar
¾ cup milk
½ cup Bisquick mix
2 eggs
2 teaspoons butter
Streusel Mix

Preheat oven to 350° and grease a 10-inch pie plate. Mix apples and spices; spoon into pie plate. Beat remaining ingredients (except streusel) until smooth; pour over apples. Sprinkle entire batch of Streusel Mix over top. Bake 55 to 60 minutes.

Streusel Mix:

1 cup Bisquick
½ cup chopped nuts
⅓ cup packed brown sugar
3 tablespoons cold margarine or butter

Combine all ingredients in a bowl, mix together until crumbly.

Stephanie Owler Loudermilk, Titusville

Sydney's Homemade Pumpkin Pie

I grow Seminole heritage pumpkins from seeds that have been passed down for generations. This is my recipe for pumpkin pie using my heritage pumpkins.

2 cups cooked, pureed fresh pumpkin
¾ cup sugar
½ teaspoon salt
1½ teaspoons ground cinnamon
1 teaspoon ground ginger
½ teaspoon ground nutmeg
½ teaspoon ground cloves
3 eggs, slightly beaten
1¼ cups milk
⅔ cup evaporated milk
1 (9-inch) unbaked deep-dish pie crust with edges crimped high

Preheat oven to 400°. Combine pumpkin, sugar, salt and spices; blend in beaten eggs, milk and evaporated milk. Pour into pastry shell. (Make sure the edges of the shell have been crimped high. This is a generous amount of pie filling; you don't want to spill it as you place it on the oven rack.) Bake 50 minutes or until a knife in the center comes out clean. Cool before cutting.

Sydney Liebman

Peter Thliveros's Southern Royalty

In Florida, you can never go wrong serving peaches for dessert. This flavorful dish is the perfect ending after a meal of red snapper with angel hair pasta. To fry the tortillas, you will need 2 (4-inch) strainers with handles bent straight up.

—Peter Thliveros, avid cook and professional bass angler on the Walmart FLW Tour

Toasted Pecans:
2 tablespoons butter
½ cup whole pecans

Melt butter in a frying pan. Add pecans and toss over medium heat until toasted. Set aside.

Tortillas:
Oil for frying
4 teaspoons ground cinnamon
4 teaspoons sugar
4 small flour tortillas

Heat enough oil in a pot to submerge strainers for deep-frying tortillas. Mix cinnamon and sugar together; set aside. Fit a tortilla into 1 strainer and place the second strainer over tortilla fitting it inside the first strainer. Submerge tortilla into hot oil. Fry until light brown and crispy. Remove from oil and place on paper towels to drain. While still warm, dust both sides with cinnamon sugar. Set aside. Repeat with remaining tortillas.

Peaches:
3 fresh peaches (or 1 pound frozen)
2 tablespoons butter
1 cup packed light brown sugar
2 jiggers Crown Royal
Vanilla ice cream

If using fresh peaches, wash, peel and pit. Cut into wedges. If using frozen peaches, simply defrost and drain excess liquid. Melt butter in a medium-size frying pan. Add sugar and cook slowly until caramelized. Add peaches and Crown Royal. Bring to a simmering bubble. If using fresh peaches, simmer until tender. If using frozen, simmer until heated through. Add Toasted Pecans. Heat about 2 minutes longer then remove from heat. Place each tortilla into 1 of 4 bowls. Scoop vanilla ice cream into tortilla shell. Spoon peach mixture with sauce over ice cream and serve immediately.

Peter Thliveros, St. Augustine
Fishing League Worldwide

Apple & Caramel Pie Bars

All my friends and family love this dish. It's a tart, shortbread-bottomed dessert this is easy to make—a winner.

Shortbread Bottom Crust:
- 4 sticks unsalted butter, softened
- ¾ cup sugar
- ½ cup packed light brown sugar
- 2 teaspoons vanilla extract
- 4 cups flour
- 1½ teaspoons salt
- ½ cup coarsely chopped pecans
- 1 teaspoon ground cinnamon

Preheat oven 375°. Using a mixer on medium speed, cream butter, sugars and vanilla until light and fluffy. In a separate bowl, combine, flour and salt. Gradually add flour mixture to creamed mixture; mixing well. Line a 9x13-inch baking pan, bottom and sides, with parchment paper. Lightly hand scatter two thirds of the dough into the pan; hand press to bottom and sides. Refrigerate prepared dough in pan 20 minutes to set. Bake 18 to 20 minutes until shortbread crust is golden brown; cool. While crust is cooling, combine the remaining dough with pecans and cinnamon; set aside.

Apple Pie Filling with Caramel Syrup:
- 4 large, ripe Granny Smith apples, peeled, quartered, cored and coarse chopped
- 4 large, ripe Golden Delicious apples, peeled, quartered, cored and coarse chopped
- 4 tablespoons freshly squeezed lemon juice
- ⅓ cup sugar
- 3 teaspoons ground cinnamon
- 2 teaspoons ground nutmeg
- ½ stick butter

In a bowl, combine apples and lemon juice; mix. Add sugar, cinnamon and nutmeg; mix well. Using a 10-inch saucepan over medium heat, melt butter; add apples. Cook 10 to 15 minutes, stirring often, until juice has somewhat evaporated. Reduce oven to 350°. Spoon cooked apples, reserving syrup, over shortbread crust leaving a ½-inch border. By hand, squeeze reserved flour dough to make crumbles and drop on top of apple mixture. Drizzle syrup on top. Bake 25 to 30 minutes or until top is browned. Cool; cut into squares. Enjoy.

Joan Barr Parker, Fernandina Beach

Rustic Florida Blueberry Cobbler

Filling:
- 1 stick butter
- 1 teaspoon lemon juice
- 4 cups fresh Florida blueberries, rinsed and drained
- 1 cup natural sugar

Topping:
- 1 cup self-rising flour
- 1 cup natural sugar
- 1 teaspoon natural vanilla extract
- ½ cup low-fat milk

Preheat oven to 375°. Place butter in an 8x8-inch glass baking dish (no substitutes) and melt in the microwave. In a mixing bowl, combine lemon juice and blueberries. Add sugar and mix well. Pour blueberry mixture in baking dish with the melted butter. Do not stir. Make topping by combining all topping ingredients in a small bowl. Pour mixture over blueberries and bake 45 minutes or until brown. Serve with fresh whipped cream or vanilla ice cream, if desired.

www.freshfromflorida.com

The Arc of the Emerald Coast Blueberry Bash

Milton • Last Weekend in June

Come out to The Arc of the Emerald Coast Blueberry Bash to enjoy blueberry picking, a plants and blueberry sale, a 5K run, foods and craft vendors, live entertainment, kids' activities, a show and shine car show, and more. All proceeds benefit The Arc of the Emerald Coast Santa Rosa.

6225 Dixie Road • Milton, FL 32570
850-982-1943 • www.arcemeraldcoast.org
Facebook: ArcEmeraldCoast

Apple Cobbler

6 apples, peeled, cored and sliced
½ teaspoon ground cinnamon or to taste
2¾ cups sugar, divided
2 cups flour
2 teaspoons baking powder
2 eggs, beaten
1 stick butter, melted

Cover bottom of a 9x13-inch greased baking pan with sliced apples. Combine cinnamon and ¾ cup sugar; sprinkle over apples. Make crumb mix by combining remaining 2 cups sugar, flour and baking powder; add eggs, stirring with a fork until mixture is the texture of cornmeal. Sprinkle evenly over apples. Spoon melted butter over top. Bake at 375° for 35 to 40 minutes. Happy baking.

Gloria Szymanski, snowbird in Fort Myers

Guava Cobbler

Cobbler:
1 stick butter
2½ cups chopped guavas
¾ cup sugar
¾ cup flour
2 teaspoons baking powder
½ teaspoon salt
¾ cup milk

Preheat oven to 325°. Melt butter in 9-inch square pan. Add guavas and stir to coat with butter. Combine sugar, flour, baking powder, salt and milk. Pour batter over guavas; do not stir. Bake 45 minutes.

Sauce:
⅔ cup chopped guavas
2 tablespoons sugar
¼ cup water
2 teaspoons cornstarch

Heat all ingredients in saucepan over medium heat until well blended. Pour warm sauce over warm cake and serve warm.

Banana Pudding with Praline Crunch

Praline Crunch:
1½ cups sugar
½ teaspoon baking soda
½ cup buttermilk
1 cup whole pecans
1 stick butter
1 teaspoon vanilla extract

In a large saucepan over medium-high heat, combine sugar, baking soda, and buttermilk. Cook, stirring constantly, until mixture reaches 228° on candy thermometer. Add pecans and butter; continue cooking to 236°. Remove from heat; add vanilla. Beat with a wooden spoon about 2 minutes or until mixture is just beginning to thicken. Drop by heaping tablespoonfuls onto parchment paper. Cool completely. Crush enough to measure 1 cup.

Banana Pudding:
2 (5.1-ounce) packages French vanilla instant pudding plus ingredients to prepare
2 (8-ounce) containers Cool Whip, divided
1 (16-ounce) box vanilla wafers
6 bananas, sliced
1 cup Praline Crunch
Chopped pecans for garnish

Prepare pudding per package directions using ½ cup less milk than directed. Combine with 1 container Cool Whip. In a large serving dish, layer half each of the wafers, sliced bananas, pudding mixture and Praline Crunch; repeat layers. Top with remaining container of Cool Whip and chopped pecans for garnish.

Mucho Mango Bread Pudding with Rum Sauce

6 slices bread, torn into small pieces
2 Florida mangoes, peeled, seeded and diced into medium-size pieces
¼ cup natural sugar
3 Florida eggs, lightly beaten
2 cups low-fat milk
1½ teaspoons natural vanilla extract
1½ teaspoons ground cardamom
2 tablespoons butter

Preheat oven to 350°. Lightly butter a 9x11-inch glass baking dish. Toss bread pieces and mango together; pour into buttered baking dish. In a medium bowl, whisk sugar, eggs, milk, vanilla and cardamom. Pour over bread and mango mixture. Place small pats of butter on top. Bake 45 to 50 minutes or until slightly puffed and golden brown. Serve warm with ice cream and fresh, sliced mangoes. Drizzle Rum Sauce over the top.

Rum Sauce:

2 tablespoons butter
½ cup natural sugar
1 tablespoon cornstarch
1 cup low-fat milk
3 tablespoons rum

Melt butter in a small saucepan over medium heat. Combine sugar and cornstarch; stir into melted butter. Slowly pour in milk, stirring frequently until mixture begins to lightly boil. Continue cooking until thick, stirring constantly. Remove from heat and stir in rum. Serve warm.

TIP: You can use any kind of sweet bread, cake or doughnuts to make the pudding. Any fruit can be used as well.

www.freshfromflorida.com

Baked Pineapple Dessert

This Baked Pineapple Dessert is best served warm. It is delicious with a dash of whipped cream or even ice cream.

½ cup butter, softened
¾ cup sugar
Salt
3 large eggs, beaten
1 (20-ounce) can crushed pineapple with juice
5 slices bread with crust, cubed

Preheat oven to 325°. Using an electric mixer on high speed, cream butter, sugar, and a dash of salt. Add eggs and beat until well mixed. Fold in pineapple (including juice) and bread cubes. Spoon into a 2-quart baking dish treated with nonstick spray. Bake 40 to 50 minutes until set. Cool about 10 minutes and serve warm.

Joan Woda, Margate

Banana Split Layered Dessert

2 cups graham cracker crumbs
1 stick butter, softened
1 (16-ounce) box powdered sugar
1 (8-ounce) package cream cheese, softened
1 egg
4 to 6 bananas, sliced
1 (20-ounce) can crushed pineapple, drained
1 (16-ounce) container Cool Whip
½ cup slivered almonds for garnish
½ cup Maraschino cherries for garnish

Mix graham cracker crumbs with butter and press into an 8x11-inch glass dish. Using an electric mixer, combine powdered sugar, cream cheese and egg. Beat together until smooth. Carefully pour over graham cracker crumbs. Top with bananas then drained pineapple. Top with Cool Whip. Refrigerate until ready to serve. Before serving, garnish with slivered almonds and drained cherries.

Blueberry Crisp

1 (20-ounce) can plus 1 (8-ounce) can crushed pineapple, undrained
3 cups fresh or frozen blueberries
¾ cup plus ¼ cup sugar, divided
1 box yellow cake mix
¼ pound butter, melted
1 cup or more chopped pecans

Preheat oven to 350°. Lightly grease 9x13-inch baking dish. Spread pineapple over bottom of pan. Add blueberries and ¾ cup sugar. Sprinkle cake mix on top of blueberries, then drizzle melted butter over top. Top with pecans and remaining sugar. Bake 25 minutes; with a spoon, cut down through cake to bottom and spread apart about 1½ inches. This will allow juice to come up through cake. Bake 35 minutes longer. Enjoy.

The Arc of the Emerald Coast Blueberry Bash
Milton Aktion Club
Captain Walt Reese, United States Navy (Retired)

Peach Crisp

5 peaches, peeled and sliced
1 cup all-purpose flour
1 cup sugar
1 teaspoon baking powder
1 teaspoon allspice
1 large egg
⅓ cup butter, melted
½ cup chopped walnuts

Preheat oven to 350°. Line a greased 8x8-inch baking dish with peach slices. Sift dry ingredients together and work in egg with pastry blender until mixture is like cornmeal. Sprinkle over peach slices. Drizzle butter and nuts on top. Bake 45 minutes.

Vanilla Bean Crème Brûlée

I am not known for my desserts, but this one is a hit. I've made it more times than I can count.

2 cups whipping cream
½ cup sugar plus ¼ cup sugar, divided
1 vanilla bean

5 large egg yolks, beaten
Sliced tropical fruit of choice

Preheat oven to 325°. Place 6 (4-inch-diameter) fluted flan dishes in 2 (9x13-inch) baking pans. In a medium saucepan, mix cream and ½ cup sugar. Split vanilla bean lengthwise, scraping seeds from inside; add bean and seeds to pan. Stir over medium heat until sugar dissolves and mixture comes to a simmer. Cover pan; reduce heat to very low. Simmer gently 10 minutes; strain into large measuring cup. Gradually whisk egg yolks into hot cream mixture; divide among dishes. Pour enough hot water into baking pans to come halfway up sides of flan dishes. Carefully transfer pans to oven; bake 30 minutes or until almost set when shaken. Cool 30 minutes; refrigerate at least 3 hours or up to 2 days. Remove custard from refrigerator and sprinkle each with 2 teaspoons sugar. Using a blowtorch, direct flame 2 inches from top to melt and brown the sugar. Refrigerate 2 hours, no longer; custard should be cool and top brittle. Garnish with fruit. Serves 6.

Sue Dannahower, Fort Pierce

Frozen Piña Colada Bites

This recipe is inspired by the trip my husband and I took to the Bahamas. Once home, I needed an alcohol-free way to relive the trip, and these Frozen Piña Colada Bites were born. They are a cross between a piña colada and a Key lime pie (because of the crust)—a match made in heaven.

Crust:

½ cup rolled oats (gluten free)
5 Medjool dates, pitted
⅛ teaspoon salt
1 tablespoon coconut oil plus more as needed

Piña Colada Filling:

½ cup mashed avocado
½ cup crushed pineapple
¼ cup melted coconut oil
¼ cup shredded coconut

Grease a mini muffin tin well with extra coconut oil (or line them with silicone muffin cups). Blend oats, dates, salt and 1 tablespoon coconut oil. Press a rounded ½ teaspoon of crust mixture into each well of the mini muffin tin. Combine Pina Colada Filling ingredients until smooth. (Blend more for a smoother consistency or less for more texture.) Spoon evenly over crust layer. Freeze. Serve frozen or remove to refrigerator 5 to 10 minutes to thaw slightly. Makes 12 servings.

Dawn Hutchins, St. Johns
Florida Coastal Cooking & Wellness

Featured Florida Festivals

January
Apalachicola Oyster Cook-Off 59
Fellsmere Frog Leg Festival 166
Florida Keys Seafood Festival 42

February
Orlando Chili Cook-Off 155
South Florida Garlic Fest 133
Steinhatchee Fiddler Crab Festival 116

March
Barberville Strawberry Fest 71
Clewiston Sugar Festival 205
Family Salsa Festival 81
Floral City Strawberry Festival 83
Florida Blueberry Festival 77
Florida Strawberry Festival 177
Fort Myers Beach Lions Club Shrimp Festival 33
GastroFest 125
Grant Seafood Festival 66
Heintz & Becker De Soto Seafood Festival 64
International Cuban Sandwich Festival 41
Lakeridge Winery's Wine & Seafood Festival 233
Original Marathon Seafood Festival 120
St. Augustine Lions Seafood Festival 111
Sandy Shoes Seafood Festival 218
Strawberry Fest of Clay County 48
Suncoast BBQ & Bluegrass Bash 170
Taste of Oviedo's Citrus & Celery Cook-Off 206
Wellington Bacon & Bourbon Fest 14

April
Bradford County Strawberry Festival 179
Fort Pierce Oyster Festival 209
Titusville Strawberry Fest 168

May
Dania Beach Arts & Seafood Celebration 160
Deering Seafood Festival 165
Isle of Eight Flags Shrimp Festival and Pirate Parade 159
Smokin' Blues, Boats, Bikes & BBQ 137

June
Arc of the Emerald Coast Blueberry Bash 227

July
Dunedin Orange Festival 13
The Key Lime Festival 222

September
Pensacola Seafood Festival 75

October
Central Florida Peanut Festival 210
Tampa Bay's Tailgate Taste Fest 19

November
Florida Seafood Festival 143

People & Places Index

Y

Recipe Index

More Great American Books

My State Notebook Series

$14.95 • 192 pages • 5⅜ x 8¼ • wire-o-bound

Alabama • Georgia • Mississippi

Busy Moms: A Farm to Table Fabulous Cookbook

$18.95 • 256 pages • 7x9
paperbound • full color

Farm to Table Fabulous

$18.95 • 248 pages • 7x9
paperbound • full color

Church Recipes are the Best

Georgia Church Suppers

$18.95 • 256 pages • 7x10 • paperbound • full color

Mississippi Church Suppers

$21.95 • 288 pages • 7x10 • paperbound • full color

Little Gulf Coast Seafood Cookbook

$14.95 • 192 pages • 5½x8½
paperbound • full color

Ultimate Venison Cookbook for Deer Camp

$21.95 • 288 pages • 7x10
paperbound • full color

Game for All Seasons Cookbook

$16.95 • 240 pages
7x10 • paperbound

Kids in the Kitchen

$18.95 • 256 pages
7x10 • paperbound • full color

Great American Grilling

$21.95 • 288 pages • 7x10
paperbound • full color

Eat & Explore State Cookbook Series

Discover community celebrations and unique destinations, as they share their favorite recipes.

EACH: $18.95 • 256 pages • 7x9 • paperbound • full color

Arkansas • Illinois • North Carolina
Ohio • Oklahoma • Virginia

State Back Road Restaurants Series

Every Road Leads to Delicious Food

EACH: $18.95 • 256 pages • 7x9
paperbound • full-color

Alabama • Kentucky • Louisiana
Missouri • North Carolina • Oklahoma
South Carolina • Tennessee • Texas

State Hometown Cookbook Series
A Hometown Taste of America, One State at a Time

Each state's hometown charm is revealed through local recipes from real hometown cooks along with stories and photos that will take you back to your hometown . . . or take you on a journey to explore other hometowns across the country.

EACH: $18.95 & $21.95* • 256 pages • 7x10
paperbound • full-color

Alabama	Louisiana	Tennessee
Florida*	Mississippi	Texas
Georgia	South Carolina	West Virginia

---

3 Easy Ways to Order

1) Call toll-free **1-888-854-5954** to order by phone or to request a free catalog.

2) Order online at **www.GreatAmericanPublishers.com**

3) Mail a check or money order for the cost of the book(s) plus $5 shipping for the first book and $1 each additional plus a list of the books you want to order along with your name, address, phone and email to:

Great American Publishers
171 Lone Pine Church Road
Lena, MS 39094

Find us on facebook: www.facebook.com/GreatAmericanPublishers

Join the **We Love 2 Cook Club** and get a 10% discount.
www.GreatAmericanPublishers.com